Lyman Beecher

Six sermons on the nature, occasions, signs, evils, and remedy of intemperance

Tenth Edition

Lyman Beecher

Six sermons on the nature, occasions, signs, evils, and remedy of intemperance
Tenth Edition

ISBN/EAN: 9783744744911

Printed in Europe, USA, Canada, Australia, Japan

Cover: Foto ©Lupo / pixelio.de

More available books at **www.hansebooks.com**

ON

THE NATURE, OCCASIONS, SIGNS, EVILS, AND REMEDY

OF

INTEMPERANCE.

BY LYMAN BEECHER, D. D.

TENTH EDITION.

PUBLISHED BY THE
AMERICAN TRACT SOCIETY,
150 NASSAU STREET, NEW-YORK.

1833.

DISTRICT OF MASSACHUSETTS......TO WIT:
District Clerk's Office.

BE it remembered, that on the twenty-third day of May, A. D. 1827, in the fifty-first year of the Independence of the United States of America, THEOPHILUS R. MARVIN, of the said District, has deposited in this Office the Title of a Book, the Right whereof he claims as Proprietor, in the Words following, to wit:

"Six Sermons on the Nature, Occasions, Signs, Evils, and Remedy of Intemperance. By Lyman Beecher, D. D."

In conformity to the Act of the Congress of the United States, entitled "An Act for the encouragement of learning, by securing the copies of maps, charts, and books, to the authors and proprietors of such copies, during the times therein mentioned;" and also to an Act entitled "An Act supplementary to an Act, entitled An Act for the encouragement of learning, by securing the copies of maps, charts, and books to the authors and proprietors of such copies during the times therein mentioned; and extending the benefits thereof to the arts of designing, engraving, and etching, historical and other prints."

JNO. W. DAVIS, } *Clerk of the District of Massachusetts.*

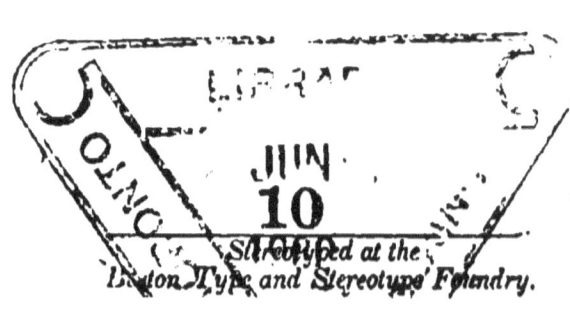

CONTENTS.

SERMON I.
The Nature and Occasions of Intemperance............ 5

SERMON II.
The Signs of Intemperance............................... 25

SERMON III.
The Evils of Intemperance............................... 47

SERMON IV.
The Remedy of Intemperance............................ 61

SERMON V.
The Remedy of Intemperance............................ 75

SERMON VI.
The Remedy of Intemperance............................ 89

SERMON I.

THE NATURE AND OCCASIONS OF INTEMPERANCE.

PROVERBS, xxiii. 29—35.

Who hath wo? who hath sorrow? who hath contentions? who hath babbling? who hath wounds without cause? who hath redness of eyes?

They that tarry long at the wine; they that go to seek mixed wine.

Look not thou upon the wine when it is red, when it giveth his colour in the cup, when it moveth itself aright. At the last it biteth like a serpent, and stingeth like an adder. Thine eye shall behold strange women, and thine heart shall utter perverse things. Yea, thou shalt be as he that lieth down in the midst of the sea, or as he that lieth upon the top of a mast. They have stricken me, shalt thou say, and I was not sick; they have beaten me, and I felt it not: when shall I awake? I will seek it yet again.

This is a glowing description of the sin of intemperance. None but the pencil of inspiration, could have thrown upon the canvass so many and such vivid traits of this complicated evil, in so short a compass. It exhibits its woes and sorrows, contentions and babblings, and wounds and redness of eyes; its smiling deceptions in the beginning, and serpent-bite in the end; the helplessness of its victims, like one cast out upon the deep; the danger of destruction, like that of one who sleeps upon the top of a mast:

the unavailing lamentations of the captive, and the giving up of hope and effort. "They have stricken me, and I was not sick; they have beaten me, and I felt it not: when shall I awake? I will seek it yet again;" again be stricken and beaten; again float upon the deep, and sleep upon the mast.

No sin has fewer apologies than intemperance. The suffrage of the world is against it; and yet there is no sin so naked in its character, and whose commencement and progress is indicated by so many signs, concerning which there is among mankind such profound ignorance. All reprobate drunkenness; and yet, not one of the thousands who fall into it, dreams of danger when he enters the way that leads to it.

The soldier, approaching the deadly breach, and seeing rank after rank of those who preceded him swept away, hesitates sometimes, and recoils from certain death. But men behold the effects upon others, of going in given courses, they see them begin, advance, and end, in confirmed intemperance, and unappalled rush heedlessly upon the same ruin.

A part of this heedlessness arises from the undefined nature of the crime in its early stages, and the ignorance of men, concerning what may be termed the experimental indications of its approach. Theft and falsehood are definite actions. But intemperance is a state of internal sensation, and the indications may exist long, and multiply, and the subject of them not be aware that they are the signs of intemperance. It is not unfrequent, that men become irreclaimable in their habits, without suspicion of danger. Nothing, therefore, seems to be more important, than a description of this broad way, thronged by so many travellers, that the temperate, when they come in sight of it, may know their danger and pass by it and turn away.

What I shall deliver on this subject, has been projected for several years, has been delayed by indisposition, and the pressure of other labors, and is advanced now without personal or local reference.

Intemperance is the sin of our land, and, with our boundless prosperity, is coming in upon us like a flood; and if anything shall defeat the hopes of the world, which hang upon our experiment of civil liberty, it is that river of fire, which is rolling through the land, destroying the vital air, and extending around an atmosphere of death.

It is proposed in this and the subsequent discourses, to consider the nature, the occasions, the signs, the evils, and the remedy of intemperance. In this discourse we shall consider

THE NATURE AND OCCASIONS OF INTEMPERANCE.

The more common apprehension is, that nothing is intemperance, which does not supersede the regular operations of the mental faculties and the bodily organs. However much a man may consume of ardent spirits, if he can command his mind, his utterance, and his bodily members, he is not reputed intemperate. And yet, drinking within these limits, he may be intemperate in respect to inordinate desire, the quantity consumed, the expense incurred, the present effect on his health and temper, and moral sensibilities, and what is more, in respect to the ultimate and inevitable results of bodily and mental imbecility, or sottish drunkenness.

God has made the human body to be sustained by food and sleep, and the mind to be invigorated by effort and the regular healthfulness of the moral system, and the cheering influence of his moral government. And whoever, to sustain the body, or invigorate the mind, or cheer the heart, applies habitually the stimulus of ardent spirits, does violence to the laws of his nature, puts the whole system into disorder, and is intemperate long before the intellect falters, or a muscle is unstrung.

The effect of ardent spirits on the brain, and the members of the body, is among the last effects of intemperance, and the least destructive part of the sin. It is the moral ruin which it works in the soul, that gives it the denomination of giant-wickedness. If all who are intemperate, drank to insensibility, and on awaking, could arise from the debauch with intellect and heart uninjured, it would strip the crime of its most appalling evils. But among the woes which the scriptures denounce against crime, one is, "wo unto them that are mighty to drink wine, and men of strength to consume strong drink." These are captains in the bands of intemperance, and will drink two generations of youths into the grave, before they go to lie down by their side. The Lord deliver us from strongheaded men, who can move the tongue when all are mute around them, and keep the eye open when all around them sleep, and can walk from the scene of riot, while their companions must be aided or wait until the morning.

It is a matter of undoubted certainty, that habitual tippling is worse than periodical drunkenness. The poor Indian, who, once a month, drinks himself *dead* all but simple breathing, will out-live for years the man who drinks little and often, and is not, perhaps, suspected of intemperance. The use of ardent spirits daily, as ministering to cheerfulness, or bodily vigor, ought to be regarded as intemperance. No person, probably, ever did, or ever will, receive ardent spirits into his system once a day, and fortify his constitution against its deleterious effects, or exercise such discretion and self government, as that the quantity will not be increased, and bodily infirmities and mental imbecility be the result, and, in more than half the instances, inebriation. Nature may hold out long against this sapping and mining of the constitution, which daily tippling is carrying on; but, first or last, this foe of life will bring to the assault enemies of its own formation, before whose power the feeble and the mighty will be alike unable to stand.

All such occasional exhilaration of the spirits by intoxicating liquors, as produces levity and foolish jesting, and the loud laugh, is intemperance, whether we regard those precepts which require us to be sober-minded, or the effect which such exhilaration and lightness has upon the cause of Christ, when witnessed in professors of religion.' The cheerfulness of health, and excitement of industry, and social intercourse, is all which nature demands, or health or purity permits.

A resort to ardent spirits as a means of invigorating the intellect, or of pleasurable sensation, is also intemperance. It is a distraint upon nature, to extort, in a short time, those results of mind and feeling, which in her own unimpelled course would flow with less impetuosity, but in a more equable and healthful current. The mind has its limits of intellectual application, and the heart its limits of feeling, and the nervous system of healthful exhilaration; and whatever you gain through stimulus, by way of anticipation, is only so much intellectual and vital power cut off at the latter end of life. It is this occult intemperance, of daily drinking, which generates a host of bodily infirmities and diseases: loss of appetite—nausea at the stomach—disordered bile—obstructions of the liver—jaundice—dropsy—hoarseness of voice—

coughs—consumptions—rheumatic pains—epilepsy—gout—colic—palsy—apoplexy—insanity—are the body-guards which attend intemperance, in the form of tippling, and where the odious name of drunkenness may perhaps be never applied.

A multitude of persons, who are not accounted drunkards, create disease, and shorten their days, by what they denominate a "prudent use of ardent spirits." Let it therefore be engraven upon the heart of every man, THAT THE DAILY USE OF ARDENT SPIRITS, IN ANY FORM, OR IN ANY DEGREE, IS INTEMPERANCE. Its effects are certain, and deeply injurious, though its results may be slow, and never be ascribed to the real cause. It is a war upon the human constitution, carried on ostensibly by an auxiliary, but which never fails to subtract more vital power than it imparts. Like the letting out of waters by little and little, the breach widens, till life itself is poured out. If all diseases which terminate in death, could speak out at the grave, or tell their origin upon the coffin-lid, we should witness the most appalling and unexpected disclosures. Happy the man, who so avoids the appearance of evil, as not to shorten his days by what he may call the prudent use of ardent spirits.

But we approach now a state of experience, in which it is supposed generally that there is some criminal intemperance. I mean when the empire of reason is invaded, and weakness and folly bear rule; prompting to garrulity, or sullen silence; inspiring petulance, or anger, or insipid good humour, and silly conversation; pouring out oaths, and curses, or opening the storehouse of secrets, their own and others. And yet, by some, all these have been thought insufficient evidence to support the charge of drinking, and to justify a process of dis' 'pline before the church. The tongue must talter, and the feet must trip, before, in the estimation of some, professors of religion can be convicted of the crime of intemperance.

To a just and comprehensive knowledge, however, of the crime of intemperance, not only a definition is required, but a philosophical analysis of its mechanical effects upon the animal system.

To those who look only on the outward appearance, the triumphs of intemperance over conscience, and talents, and learning, and character, and interest, and family endearments, have appeared wonderful. But the wonder will cease, when we consider the raging desire which it enkindles, and the hand of torment which it lays, on every fibre of the body and faculty of the soul.

The stomach is the great organ of accelerated circulation to the blood, of elasticity to the animal spirits, of pleasurable or painful vibration to the nerves, of vigor to the mind, and of fulness to the cheerful affections of the soul. Here is the silver cord of life, and the golden bowl at the fountain, and the wheel at the cistern; and as these fulfil their duty, the muscular and mental and moral powers act in unison, and fill the system with vigor and delight. But as these central energies are enfeebled, the strength of mind and body declines, and lassitude, and depression, and melancholy, and sighing, succeed to the high beatings of health, and the light of life becomes as darkness.

Experience has decided, that any stimulus applied statedly to the stomach, which raises its muscular tone above the point at which it can be sustained by food and sleep, produces, when it has passed away, debility—a relaxation of the over-worked organ, proportioned to its preternatural excitement. The life-giving power of the stomach falls of course as much below the tone of cheerfulness and health, as it was injudiciously raised above it. If the experiment be repeated often, it produces an artificial tone of stomach, essential to cheerfulness and muscular vigor, entirely above the power of the regular sustenance of nature to sustain, and creates a vacuum, which nothing can fill, but the destructive power which made it—and when protracted use has made the difference great, between the natural and this artificial tone, and habit has made it a second nature, the man is a drunkard, and, in ninety-nine instances in a hundred, is irretrievably undone. Whether his tongue falter, or his feet fail him or not, he will die of intemperance. By whatever name his disease may be called, it will be one of the legion which lie in wait about the path of intemperance, and which abused Heaven employs to execute wrath upon the guilty.

But of all the ways to hell, which the feet of deluded mortals tread, that of the intemperate is the most dreary and terrific. The demand for artificial stimulus to supply the deficiencies of healthful aliment, is like the rage of thirst, and the ravenous demand of famine. It is famine: for the artificial excitement has become as essential now to strength and cheerfulness, as simple nutrition once was. But nature, taught by habit to require what once she did not need, demands gratification now with a decision inexorable as death, and to most men as irresistible. The denial is a living death. The stomach, the head, the heart, and arteries, and veins, and every muscle, and every nerve, feel the exhaustion, and the restless, unutterable wretchedness which puts out the light of life, and curtains the heavens, and carpets the earth with sackcloth. All these varieties of sinking nature, call upon the wretched man with trumpet tongue, to dispel this darkness, and raise the ebbing tide of life, by the application of the cause which produced these woes, and after a momentary alleviation will produce them again with deeper terrors, and more urgent importunity; for the repetition, at each time renders the darkness deeper, and the torments of self-denial more irresistible and intolerable.

At length, the excitability of nature flags, and

stimulants of higher power, and in greater quantities, are required to rouse the impaired energies of life, until at length the whole process of dilatory murder, and worse than purgatorial suffering, having been passed over, the silver cord is loosed, the golden bowl is broken, the wheel at the cistern stops, and the dust returns to the earth as it was, and the spirit to God who gave it.

These sufferings, however, of animal nature, are not to be compared with the moral agonies which convulse the soul. It is an immortal being who sins, and suffers; and as his earthly house dissolves, he is approaching the judgment seat, in anticipation of a miserable eternity. He feels his captivity, and in anguish of spirit clanks his chains and cries for help. Conscience thunders, remorse goads, and as the gulf opens before him, he recoils, and trembles, and weeps, and prays, and resolves, and promises, and reforms, and "seeks it yet again,"—again resolves, and weeps, and prays, and " seeks it yet again!" Wretched man, he has placed himself in the hands of a giant, who never pities, and never relaxes his iron gripe. He may struggle, but he is in chains. He may cry for release, but it comes not; and lost! lost! may be inscribed upon the door posts of his dwelling.

In the mean time these paroxysms of his dying moral nature decline, and a fearful apathy, the harbinger of spiritual death, comes on. His resolution fails, and his mental energy, and his vigorous enterprise; and nervous irritation and depression ensue. The social affections lose their fulness and tenderness, and conscience loses its power, and the heart its sensibility, until all that was once lovely and of good report, retires and leaves the wretch abandoned to the appetites of a ruined animal. In this deplorable condition, reputation expires, business falters and becomes perplexed, and temptations to drink multiply as inclination to do so increases, and the power of resistance declines. And now the vortex roars, and the struggling victim buffets the fiery wave with feebler stroke, and warning supplication, until despair flashes upon his soul, and with an outcry that pierces the heavens, he ceases to strive, and disappears.

A sin so terrific should be detected in its origin and strangled in the cradle; but ordinarily, instead of this, the habit is fixed, and the hope of reformation is gone, before the subject has the least suspicion of danger. It is of vast importance therefore, that the various occasions of intemperance should be clearly described, that those whose condition is not irretrievable, may perceive their danger, and escape, and that all who are free, may be warned off from these places of temptation and ruin. For the benefit of the young, especially, I propose to lay down a map of the way to destruction, and to rear a monument of warning upon every spot where a wayfaring man has been ensnared and destroyed.

The first occasion of intemperance which I shall mention, is found in the free and frequent use of ardent spirits in the family, as an incentive to appetite, an alleviation of lassitude, or an excitement to cheerfulness. In these reiterated indulgences, children are allowed to partake, and the tender organs of their stomachs are early perverted, and predisposed to habits of intemperance. No family, it is believed, accustomed to the daily use of ardent spirits, ever failed to plant the seeds of that dreadful disease, which sooner or later produced a harvest of wo. The material of so much temptation and mischief, ought not to be allowed a place in the family, except only as a medicine, and even then it would be safer in the hands of the apothecary, to be sent for like other medicine, when prescribed.

Ardent spirits, given as a matter of hospitality, is not unfrequently the occasion of intemperance. In this case the temptation is a stated inmate of the family. The utensils are present, and the occasions for their use are not unfrequent. And when there is no guest, the sight of the liquor, the state of the health, or even lassitude of spirits, may indicate the propriety of the "prudent use," until the prudent use becomes, by repetition, habitual use—and habitual use becomes irreclaimable intemperance. In this manner, doubtless, has many a father, and mother, and son, and daughter, been ruined forever.

Of the guests, also, who partake in this family hospitality, the number is not small, who become ensnared; especially among those whose profession calls them to visit families often, and many on the same day. Instead of being regarded, therefore, as an act of hospitality, and a token of friendship, to invite our friends to drink, it ought to be regarded as an act of incivility, to place ourselves and them in circumstances of such high temptation.

Days of public convocation are extensively the occasions of excess which eventuate in intemperance. The means and temptations are ostentatiously multiplied, and multitudes go forth prepared and resolved to yield to temptation, while example and exhilarated feeling secure the ample fulfilment of their purpose.—But when the habit is once acquired of drinking even "*prudently,*" as it will be called, on all the days of public convocation which occur in a year, a desire will be soon formed of drinking at other times, until the healthful appetite of nature is superseded by the artificial thirst produced by ardent spirits.

Evening resorts for conversation, enlivened by the cheering bowl, have proved fatal to thousands. Though nothing should be boisterous, and all should seem only the "feast of reason, and the flow of soul," yet at the latter end it biteth like a serpent and stingeth like an adder: many a wretched man has shaken his chains and cried out in the anguish of his spirit, oh!

that accursed resort of social drinking; there my hands were bound and my feet put in fetters; there I went a freeman and became a slave, a temperate man and became a drunkard.

In the same class of high temptation are to be ranked all convivial associations for the purpose of drinking, with or without gambling, and late hours. There is nothing which young men of spirit fear less, than the exhilaration of drinking on such occasions, nor any thing which they are less able to resist, than the charge of cowardice when challenged to drink. But there is no one form of temptation before which more young men of promise have fallen into irretrievable ruin. The connexion between such beginnings and a fatal end is so manifest, and the presumptuous daring of Heaven is so great, that God in his righteous displeasure is accustomed to withdraw his protection and abandon the sinner to his own way.

Feeble health and mental depression are to be numbered among the occasions of intemperance. The vital sinking, and muscular debility, and mental darkness, are for a short time alleviated by the application of stimulants. But the cause of this momentary alleviation is applied and repeated, until the habit of excessive drinking is formed and has become irresistible.

Medical prescriptions have no doubt contributed to increase the number of the intemperate. Ardent spirits, administered in the form of bitters, or as the medium of other medicine, have let in the destroyer; and while the patient was seeking health at the hand of the physician, he was dealing out debility and death.

The distillation of ardent spirits fails not to raise up around the establishment a generation of drunkards. The cheapness of the article, and the ease with which families can provide themselves with large quantities, the product of their own labor, eventuate in frequent drinking, and wide spread intemperance.

The vending of ardent spirits, in places licensed or unlicensed, is a tremendous evil. Here, those who have no stated employment loiter away the day for a few potations of rum, and here, those who have finished the toils of the day meet to spend a vacant hour; none content to be lookers on: all drink, and none for any length of time drink temperately. Here too the children of a neighborhood, drawn in by enticements, associate for social drinking, and the exhibition of courage and premature manhood. And here the iron hand of the monster is fastened upon them, at a period when they ought not to have been beyond the reach of maternal observation.

The continued habit of dealing out ardent spirits, in various forms and mixtures, leads also to frequent tasting, and tasting to drinking, and drinking to tippling, and tippling to drunkenness.

A resort to ardent spirits as an alleviation of trouble, results often in habits of confirmed intemperance. The loss of friends, perplexities of business, or the wreck of property, bring upon the spirits the distractions of care and the pressure of sorrow; and, instead of casting their cares upon the Lord, they resort to the exhilarating draught, but, before the occasion for it has ceased, the remedy itself has become a calamity more intolerable than the disease. Before, the woes were temporary; now, they have multiplied and have become eternal.

Ardent spirits employed to invigorate the intellect, or restore exhausted nature under severe study, is often a fatal experiment. Mighty men have been cast down in this manner never to rise. The quickened circulation does for a time invigorate intellect and restore exhausted nature. But, for the adventitious energy imparted, it exhausts the native energy of the soul, and induces that faintness of heart, and flagging of the spirits, which cry incessantly, "give, give," and never, but with expiring breath, say it is enough.

The use of ardent spirits, employed as an auxiliary to labor, is among the most fatal, because the most common and least suspected, causes of intemperance. It is justified as innocent, it is insisted on as necessary: but no fact is more completely established by experience than that it is utterly useless, and ultimately injurious, beside all the fearful evils of habitual intemperance, to which it so often leads. THERE IS NO NUTRITION IN ARDENT SPIRIT. ALL THAT

IT DOES IS, TO CONCENTRATE THE STRENGTH OF THE SYSTEM FOR THE TIME, BEYOND ITS CAPACITY FOR REGULAR EXERTION. It is borrowing strength for an occasion, which will be needed for futurity, without any provision for payment, and with the certainty of ultimate bankruptcy.

The early settlers of New-England endured more hardship, and performed more labor, and carried through life more health and vigor, than appertains to the existing generation of laboring men. And they did it without the use of ardent spirits.

Let two men, of equal age and firmness of constitution, labor together through the summer, the one with and the other without the excitement of ardent spirits, and the latter will come out at the end with unimpaired vigor, while the other will be comparatively exhausted. Ships navigated as some now are without the habitual use of ardent spirits—and manufacturing establishments carried on without—and extended agricultural operations—all move on with better industry, more peace, more health, and a better income to the employers and the employed. The workmen are cheerful and vigorous, friendly and industrious, and their families are thrifty, well fed, well clothed and instructed; and instead of distress and poverty, and disappointment and contention—they are cheered with the full flow of social affection, and often by the sustaining power of religion. But where ardent spirit is received as a daily auxiliary to labor, it is commonly taken at stated times—the habit soon creates a vacancy in the stomach, which indicates at length the hour of the day with as much accuracy as a clock. It will be taken besides, frequently, at other times, which will accelerate the destruction of nature's healthful tone, create artificial debility, and the necessity of artificial excitement to remove it; and when so much has been consumed as the economy of the employer can allow, the growing demand will be supplied by the evening and morning dram, from the wages of labor—until the appetite has become insatiable, and the habit of intemperance nearly universal—until the nervous excitability has obliterated the social sensibilities, and turned the family into a scene of babbling and wo—until voracious appetite has eaten up the children's bread, and abandoned them to ignorance and crime—until conscience has become callous, and fidelity and industry have disappeared, except as the result of eye service; and wanton wastefulness and contention, and reckless wretchedness characterize the establishment.

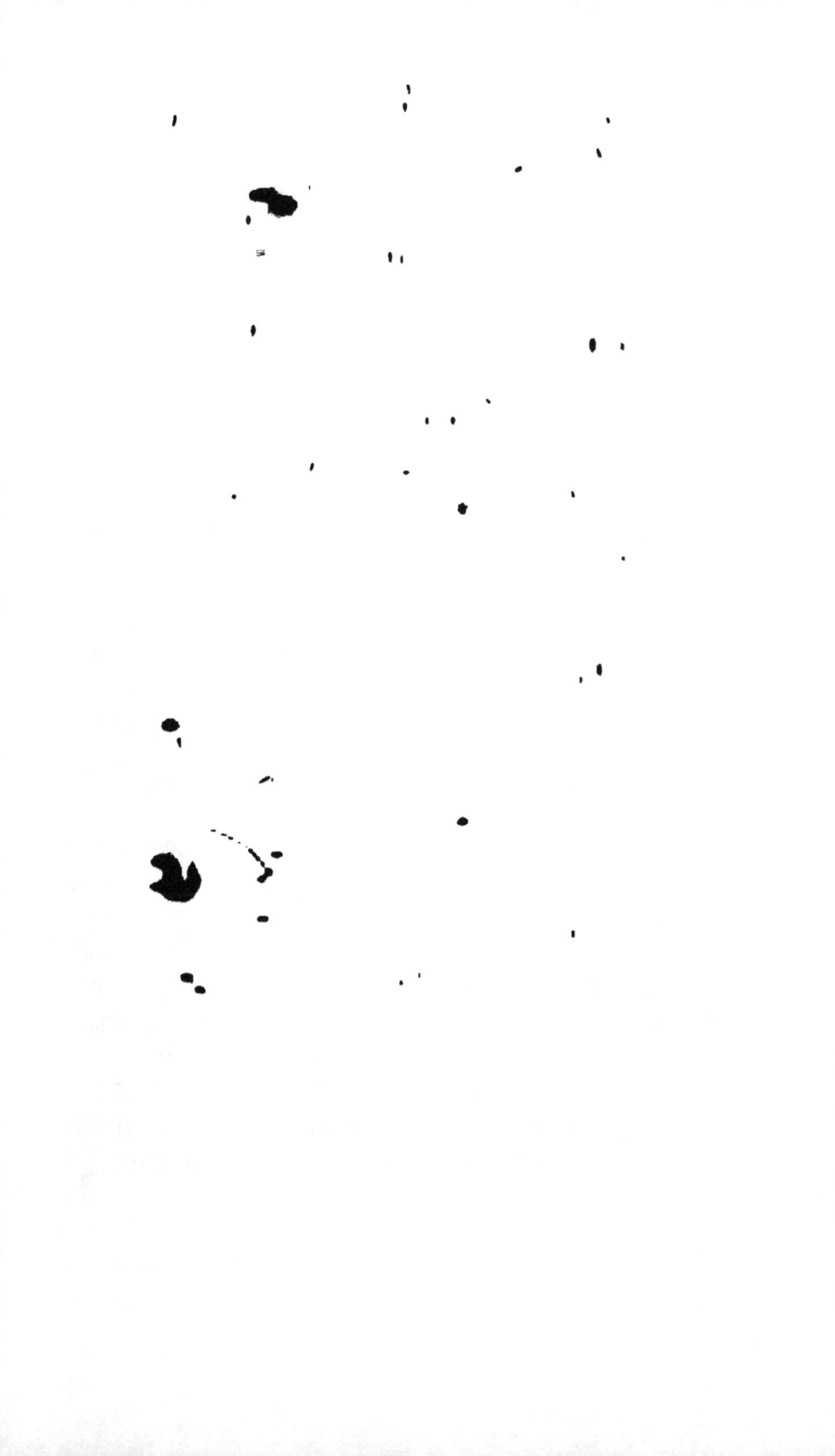

SERMON II.

THE SIGNS OF INTEMPERANCE.

PROVERBS, xxiii. 29--35.

Who hath wo? who hath sorrow? who hath contentions? who hath babbling? who hath wounds without cause? who hath redness of eyes?

They that tarry long at the wine; they that go to seek mixed wine.

Look not thou upon the wine when it is red, when it giveth his colour in the cup, when it moveth itself aright. At the last it biteth like a serpent, and stingeth like an adder. Thine eye shall behold strange women, and thine heart shall utter perverse things. Yea, thou shalt be as he that lieth down in the midst of the sea, or as he that lieth upon the top of a mast. They have stricken me, shalt thou say, and I was not sick; they have beaten me, and I felt it not: when shall I awake? I will seek it yet again.

In the preceding discourse I considered the nature and occasions of intemperance. In this I shall disclose some of the symptoms of this fearful malady, as they affect both the body and the mind, that every one, who is in any degree addicted to the sin, may be apprised of his danger, and save himself before it be too late.

In the early stages of intemperance reformation is practicable. The calamity is, that intemperance is a sin so deceitful, that most men go on to irretrievable ruin, warned indeed by many indications, but unavailingly, because they understand not their voice.

It is of vast importance, therefore, that the symptoms of intemperance should be universally and familiarly known; the effects of the sin upon the body, and upon the mind, should be so described in all its stages, from the beginning to the end, that every one may see, and feel, and recognise these harbingers of death as soon as they begin to show themselves upon him.

1. One of the early indications of intemperance may be found in the associations of time and place.

In the commencement of this evil habit, there are many who drink to excess only on particular days, such as days for military exhibition, the anniversary of our independence, the birth-day of Washington, Christmas, new year's day, election, and others of the like nature. When any of these holidays arrive, and they come as often almost as saints' days in the calendar, they bring with them, to many, the insatiable desire of drinking, as well as a dispensation from the sin, as efficacious and quieting to the conscience, as papal indulgences.

There are some I am aware that have recommended the multiplication of holidays and public amusements, as a remedy for intemperance:—about as wise a prescription—as the multiplying gambling houses to supersede gambling, or the building of theatres to correct the evils of the stage.

There are others who feel the desire of drinking stirred up within them by the associations of place. They could go from end to end of a day's journey without ardent spirits, were there no taverns on the road. But the very sight of these receptacles of pilgrims awakens the desire "just to step in and take something." And so powerful does this association become, that many will no more pass the tavern than they would pass a fortified place with all the engines of death directed against them. There are in every city, town, and village, places of resort, which in like manner, as soon as the eye falls upon them, create the thirst of drinking, and many, who, coming to market or on business, pass near them, pay toll there as regularly as they do at the gates; and sometimes both when they come in and when they go out. In cities and their suburbs, there are hundreds of shops at which a large proportion of those who bring in produce stop regularly to receive the customary beverage.

In every community you may observe particular persons also who can never meet without feeling the simultaneous desire of strong drink. What can be the reason of this? All men, when they meet, are not affected thus. It is not uncommon for men of similar employments to be drawn by association, when they meet, to the same topics of conversation:—physicians, upon the concerns of their profession:—politicians, upon the events of the day :—and Christians, when they meet, are drawn by a common interest to speak of the things of the kingdom of God. But this is upon the principle of a common interest in these subjects, which has no slight hold upon the thoughts and affections. Whoever then finds himself tempted on meeting his companion or friend to say, 'come and let us go and take something,' or, to make it his first business to set out his decanter and glasses, ought to understand that he discloses his own inordinate attachment to ardent spirits, and accuses his friend of intemperance.

2. A disposition to multiply the circumstances which furnish the occasions and opportunities for drinking, may justly create alarm that the habit is begun. When you find occasions for drinking in all the variations of the weather, because it is so hot or so cold—so wet or so dry—and in all the different states of the system—when you are vigorous, that you need not tire—and when tired, that your vigor may be restored, you have approached near to that state of intemperance in which you will drink in all states of the weather, and conditions of the body, and will drink with these pretexts, and drink without them whenever their frequency may not suffice. In like manner if, on your farm, or in your store, or workshop, or on board your vessel, you love to multiply the catches and occasions of drinking, in the forms of treats for new comers—for mistakes—for new articles of

dress—or furniture—until in some places a man can scarcely wear an article of dress, or receive one of equipage or furniture, which has not been "wet," you may rely on it that all these usages, and rules, and laws, are devices to gratify an inordinate and dangerous love of strong drink; and though the master of the shop should not himself come down to such little measures, yet if he permits such things to be done, if he hears, and sees, and smiles, and sometimes sips a little of the forfeited beverage, his heart is in the thing, and he is under the influence of a dangerous love of that hilarity which is produced by strong drink.

3. Whoever finds the desire of drinking ardent spirits returning daily at stated times, is warned to deny himself instantly, if he intends to escape confirmed intemperance.

It is infallible evidence that you have already done violence to nature—that the undermining process is begun—that the over-worked organ begins to flag, and cry out for adventitious aid, with an importunity which, if indulged, will become more deep toned, and importunate, and irresistible, until the power of self-denial is gone, and you are a ruined man. It is the vortex begun, which, if not checked, will become more capacious, and deep, and powerful, and loud, until the interests of time and eternity are engulfed.

It is here then—beside this commencing vortex—that I would take my stand, to warn off the heedless navigator from destruction. To all who do but heave in sight, and with voice that should rise above the winds and waves, I would cry—" stand off!!!"—spread the sail, ply the oar, for death is here—and could I command the elements—the blackness of darkness should gather over this gate-way to hell—and loud thunders should utter their voices—and lurid fires should blaze—and the groans of unearthly voices should be heard—inspiring consternation and flight in all who came near. For this is the parting point between those who forsake danger and hide themselves, and the foolish who pass on and are punished. He who escapes this periodical thirst of times and seasons, will not be a drunkard, as he who comes within the reach of this powerful attraction will be sure to perish. It may not be certain that every one will become a sot; but it is certain that every one will enfeeble his body, generate disease, and shorten his days. It may not be certain that every one will sacrifice his reputation, or squander his property, and die in the alms house; but it is certain that a large proportion will come to poverty and infamy, of those who yield daily to the periodical appetite for ardent spirits. Here is the stopping place, and though beyond it men may struggle, and retard, and modify their progress, none, comparatively, who go by it, will return again to purity of enjoyment, and the sweets of temperate liberty. The servant has become the master, and, with a rod of iron and a whip of scorpions, he will torment, even before their time, the candidates for misery in a future state.

4. Another sign of intemperance may be found in the desire of concealment. When a man finds himself disposed to drink oftener, and more than he is willing to do before his family and the world, and begins to drink slily and in secret places, he betrays a consciousness that he is disposed to drink more than to others will appear safe and proper, and what he *suspects* others may think, he ought to suppose they have *cause* to think, and reform instantly. For now he has arrived at a period in the history of intemperance, where, if he does not stop, he will hasten on to ruin with accelerated movement. So long as the eye of friendship and a regard to public observation kept him within limits, there was some hope of reformation; but when he cuts this last cord, and launches out alone with his boat and bottle, he has committed himself to mountain waves and furious winds, and probably will never return.

5. When a man allows himself to drink always in company so much as he may think he can bear without awakening in others the suspicion of inebriation, he will deceive himself, and no one beside. For abused nature herself will publish the excess in the bloated countenance, and flushed visage, and tainted breath, and inflamed eye; and were all these banners of intemperance struck, the man with his own tongue will reveal his shame. At first there will be

something strange in his appearance or conduct, to awaken observation, and induce scrutiny, until at length, with all his carefulness, in some unguarded moment he will take more than he can bear. And now the secret is out, and these unaccountable things are explained; these exposures will become more frequent, the unhappy man still dreaming that though he erred a little, he took such good care to conceal it, that no one knew it but himself. He will even talk when his tongue is palsied, to ward off suspicion, and thrust himself into company, to show that he is not drunk.

6. Those persons who find themselves for some cause always irritated when efforts are made to suppress intemperance, and moved by some instinctive impulse to make opposition, ought to examine instantly whether the love of ardent spirits is not the cause of it.

An aged country merchant, of an acute mind and sterling reputation, once said to me, "I never knew an attempt made to suppress intemperance, which was not opposed by some persons, from whom I should not have expected opposition; and I never failed to find, first or last, that these persons were themselves implicated in the sin." Temperate men seldom if ever oppose the reformation of intemperance.

7. We now approach some of those symptoms of intemperance which abused nature first or last never fails to give.

The eyes. Who hath redness of eyes? All

are not of course intemperate whose visual organs become inflamed and weak. But there are few intemperate persons who escape this malady, and yet when it comes, they have no suspicion of the cause—speak of it without embarrassment —and wonder what the matter can be—apply to the physician for eye water, and drink on. But every man who is accustomed to drink ardent spirits freely, whose eye begins to redden and to weep, ought to know what the matter is, and to take warning; it is one of the signals which distressed nature holds out and waves in token of distress.

Another indication of intemperance is found in the fulness and redness of the countenance. It is not the fulness and freshness of health—but rather the plethora of a relaxed fibre and peccant humours, which come to occupy the vacancy of healthful nutrition, and to mar the countenance with pimples and inflammation. All are not intemperate of course who are affected with diseases of the skin. But no hard drinker carries such a face without a guilty and specific cause, and it is another signal of distress which abused nature holds out, while she cries for help.

Another indication of intemperance may be found in impaired muscular strength and tremour of the hand. Now the destroyer, in his mining process, approaches the citadel of life, and is advancing fast to make the keepers of the house tremble, and the strong men bow themselves. This relaxation of the joints, and trembling of the nerves, will be experienced especially in the morning—when the system, unsustained by sleep, has run down. Now all is relaxed, tremulous, and faint-hearted. The fire which sparkled in the eye, the evening before, is quenched—the courage which dilated the heart is passed away—and the tones of eloquence, which dwelt on the inspired tongue, are turned into pusillanimous complainings, until opium, or bitters, or both, are thrown into the stomach to wind up again the run-down machine.

And now the liver, steeped in fire, begins to contract, and refuses to perform its functions, in preparing the secretions which are necessary to aid digestion; and loss of appetite ensues; and indigestion, and fermentation, and acidity, begin to rob the system of nutrition, and to vex and irritate the vital organ, filling the stomach with air, and the head with fumes, and the soul with darkness and terror.

This reiterated irritation extends by sympathy to the lungs, which become inflamed and lacerated, until hemorrhage ensues. And now the terrified victim hastens to the physician to stay the progress of a consumption, which intemperance has begun, and which medical treatment, while the cause continues, cannot arrest.

About this time the fumes of the scalding furnace below begin to lacerate the throat, and blister the tongue and the lip. Here again the physician is called in to ease these torments; but until the fires beneath are extinct, what can the physician do? He can no more alleviate these woes than he can carry alleviation to the tormented, in the flames for which these are the sad preparations.

Another indication of intemperance is irritability, petulance, and violent anger. The great organ of nervous sensibility has been brought into a state of tremulous excitement. The slightest touch causes painful vibrations, and irritations, which defy self-government.—The temper becomes like the flash of powder, or ungovernable and violent as the helm driven hither and thither by raging winds, and mountain waves.

Another indication of intemperance is to be found in the extinction of all the finer feelings and amiable dispositions of the soul; and, if there have ever seemed to be religious affections, of these also. The fiery stimulus has raised the organ of sensibility above the power of excitement by motives addressed to the finer feelings of the soul, and of the moral nature, and left the man a prey to animal sensation. You might as well fling out music upon the whirlwind to stay its course, as to govern the storm within by the gentler feelings of humanity. The only stimulant which now has power to move, is ardent spirits—and he who has arrived at this condition is lost. He has left far behind the wreck of what he once was. He is not the same husband, or father, or brother, or friend. The sea has made a clear breach over him, and swept away forever whatsoever things are pure, and lovely, and of good report.

And as to religion, if he ever seemed to have any, all such affections declined as the emotions of artificial stimulants arose, until conscience has lost its power, or survives only with vulture scream to flap the wing, and terrify the soul. His religious affections are dead when he is sober, and rise only to emotion and loquacity and tears when he is drunk. Dead, twice dead, is he—whatever may have been the hopes he once indulged, or the evidence he once gave, or the hopes he once inspired. For drunkards, no more than murderers, shall inherit the kingdom of God.

As the disease makes progress, rheumatic pains diffuse themselves throughout the system. The man wonders what can be the reason that he should be visited by such a complication of disease, and again betakes himself to the physician, and tries every remedy but the simple one of temperance. For these pains are only the murmurings and complainings of nature, through all the system giving signs of wo, that all is lost. For to rheumatic pains ensues a debility of the system, which becoming unable to sustain the circulation, the fluids fall first upon the feet, and, as the deluge rises, the chest is invaded, and the breath is shortened, until by a sudden inundation it is stopped. Or, if in this form death is avoided, it is only to be met in another—more dilatory but no less terrific; for now comes on the last catastrophe—the sudden prostration of strength and appetite—an increased difficulty of raising the ebbing tide of life by stimulants—a few panic struck reformations, just on the sides of the pit, until the last sinking comes, from which there is no resurrection but by the trump of God, and at the judgment day.

And now the woes, and the sorrows, and the contentions, and the wounds, and babblings, are over—the red eye sleeps—the tortured body rests—the deformed visage is hid from human observation—and the soul, while the dust crumbles back to dust, returns to God who gave it, to receive according to the deeds done in the body.

Such is the evil which demands a remedy. And what can be done to stop its ravages and rescue its victims?

This is not the place to say all that belongs to this part of the subject, but we cannot close without saying by anticipation a few things here; and,

1. There should be extended through the community an all-pervading sense of the danger there is of falling into this sin. Intemperance is a disease as well as a crime, and were any other disease, as contagious, of as marked symptoms, and as mortal, to pervade the land, it would create universal consternation: for the plague is scarcely more contagious or deadly; and yet we mingle fearlessly with the diseased, and in spite of admonition we bring into our dwellings the contagion, apply it to the lip, and receive it into the system.

I know that much is said about the prudent use of ardent spirits; but we might as well speak of the prudent use of the plague—of fire handed prudently around among powder—of poison taken prudently every day—or of vipers and serpents introduced prudently into our dwellings, to glide about as a matter of courtesy to visitors, and of amusement to our children.

First or last, in spite of your prudence, the contagion will take—the fatal spark will fall upon the train—the deleterious poison will tell upon the system—and the fangs of the serpent will inflict death. There is no prudent use of ardent spirits, but when it is used as a medicine. All who receive it into the system are not destroyed by it. But if any vegetable were poisonous to as many, as the use of ardent spirits proves destructive, it would be banished from the table; it would not be prudent to use it at all. If in attempting to cross a river upon an elastic beam—as many should fall in and be drowned, as attempt to use ardent spirits *prudently* and fail, the attempt to cross in that way would be abandoned—there would be no prudent use of that mode of crossing. The effect of attempting to use ardent spirits prudently, is destructive to such multitudes, as precludes the possibility of prudence in the use of it. When we consider the deceitful nature of this sin, and its irresistible power when it has obtained an ascendency—no man can use it prudently—or without mocking God can pray while he uses it, "lead us not into temptation." There is no necessity for using it at all, and it is presumptuous to do so.

2. A wakeful recollection should be maintained of the distinction between intemperance and drunkenness. So long as men suppose that there is neither crime nor danger in drinking, short of what they denominate drunkenness, they will cast off fear and move onward to ruin by a silent, certain course, until destruction comes upon them, and they cannot escape. It should be known therefore and admitted, that to drink daily, at stated times, any quantity of ardent spirits, is intemperance, or to drink periodically as often as days, and times, and seasons, may furnish temptation and opportunity, is intemperance. It may not be for any one time the intemperance of animal or mental excitement, but it is an innovation upon the system, and the beginning of a habit, which cannot fail to generate disease, and will not be pursued by one hundred men without producing many drunkards.

It is not enough therefore to erect the flag ahead, to mark the spot where the drunkard dies. It must be planted at the entrance of his course, proclaiming in waving capitals—THIS IS THE WAY TO DEATH!! Over the whole territory of "prudent use," it must wave and warn. For if we cannot stop men in the beginning, we cannot separate between that and the end. He who lets ardent spirits alone before it is meddled with, is safe, and he only. It should be in every family a contraband article, or if it is admitted, it should be allowed for medical purposes only. It should be labelled as we label laudanum—and TOUCH NOT, TASTE NOT, HANDLE NOT, should meet the eye on every vessel which contains it.

Children should be taught early the nature, symptoms, and danger of this sin, that they may not unwittingly fall under its power. To save my own children from this sin has been no small part of my solicitude as a parent, and I can truly say, that should any of my children perish in this way, they will not do it ignorantly, nor unwarned. I do not remember that I ever gave permission to a child to go out on a holiday, or gave a pittance of money to be expended for his gratification, unattended by the earnest injunction, not to drink ardent spirits, or any inebriating liquor; and I cannot but believe, that if proper exertions are made in the family to apprise children of the nature and danger of this sin, and to put them on their guard against it—opinions and feelings and habits might be so formed, that the whole youthful generation might rise up as a rampart, against which the fiery waves of intemperance would dash in vain, saying, hitherto shalt thou come, but no farther, and here shall thy proud waves be stayed. To all our schools instruction on this subject should be communicated, and the Sabbath schools now spreading through the land, may in this manner lend a mighty influence to prevent the intemperance of the rising generation.

In respect to the reformation of those over

whom the habit of intemperance has obtained an ascendency, there is but one alternative—they must resolve upon immediate and entire abstinence.

Some have recommended, and many have attempted, a gradual discontinuance. But no man's prudence and fortitude are equal to the task of reformation in this way. If the patient were in close confinement, where he could not help himself, he might be dealt with in this manner, but it would be cruelly protracting a course of suffering through months, which might be ended in a few days. But no man, at liberty, will reform by gradual retrenchment.—Substitutes have also been recommended as the means of reformation, such as opium, which is only another mode of producing inebriation, is often a temptation to intemperance, and not unfrequently unites its own forces with those of ardent spirits to impair health, and destroy life. It is a preternatural stimulant, raising excitement above the tone of health, and predisposing the system for intemperate drinking.

Strong beer has been recommended as a substitute for ardent spirits, and a means of leading back the captive to health and liberty. But though it may not create intemperate habits as soon, it has no power to allay them. It will finish even what ardent spirits have begun—and with this difference only, that it does not rasp the vital organs with quite so keen a file—and enables the victim to come down to his grave, by a course somewhat more dilatory, and with more of the good natured stupidity of the idiot, and less of the demoniac frenzy of the madman.

Wine has been prescribed as a means of decoying the intemperate from the ways of death. But habit cannot be thus cheated out of its dominion, nor ravening appetite be amused down to a sober and temperate demand. If it be true that men do not become intemperate on wine, it is not true that wine will restore the intemperate, or stay the progress of the disease. Enough must be taken to screw up nature to the tone of cheerfulness, or she will cry "give," with an importunity not to be resisted, and long before the work of death is done, wine will fail to minister a stimulus of sufficient activity to rouse the flagging spirits, or will become acid on the enfeebled stomach, and brandy and opium will be called in to hasten to its consummation the dilatory work of self-destruction. So that if no man becomes a sot upon wine, it is only because it hands him over to more fierce and terrible executioners of Heaven's delayed vengeance.

If in any instance wine suffices to complete the work of ruin, then the difference is only that the victim is stretched longer upon the rack, to die in torture with the gout, while ardent spirits finish life by a shorter and perhaps less painful course.

Retrenchments and substitutes then are idle, and if in any case they succeed, it is not in one of a thousand. It is the tampering of an infant with a giant, the effort of a kitten to escape from the paw of a lion.

There is no remedy for intemperance but the cessation of it. Nature must be released from the unnatural war which is made upon her, and be allowed to rest, and then nutrition, and sleep, and exercise, will perform the work of restoration. Gradually the spring of life will recover tone, appetite will return, digestion become efficient, sleep sweet, and the muscular system vigorous, until the elastic heart with every beat shall send health through the system, and joy through the soul.

But what shall be done for those to whom it might be fatal to stop short? Many are reputed to be in this condition, probably, who are not—and those who are, may, while under the care of a physician, be dealt with, as he may think best for the time, provided they obey strictly as patients his prescriptions. But if, when they are committed to their own care again, they cannot live without ardent spirits—then they must die, and have only the alternative to die as reformed penitents, or as incorrigibly intemperate—to die in a manner which shall secure pardon and admission to heaven, or in a manner which shall exclude them forever from that holy world.

As the application of this discourse, I would recommend to every one of you who hear it, immediate and faithful self-examination. to ascertain whether any of the symptoms of intemperance are beginning to show themselves upon you. And let not the consideration that you have never been suspected, and have never suspected yourselves of intemperance, deprive you of the benefit of this scrutiny. For it is inattention and self-confidence which supersede discretion, and banish fear, and let in the destroyer, to fasten upon his victim, before he thinks of danger or attempts resistance.

Are there then set times, days, and places, when you calculate always to indulge yourselves in drinking ardent spirits? Do you stop often to take something at the tavern when you travel, and always when you come to the village, town, or city. This frequency of drinking will plant in your system, before you are aware of it, the seeds of the most terrific disease which afflicts humanity. Have you any friends or companions whose presence, when you meet them, awakens the thought and the desire of drinking? Both of you have entered on a course in which there is neither safety nor hope, but from instant retreat.

Do any of you love to avail yourselves of every little catch and circumstance among your companions, to bring out "a treat?" "Alas, my lord, there is death in the pot."

Do you find the desire of strong drink returning daily, and at stated hours? Unless you intend to travel all the length of the highway of intemperance, it is time to stop. Unless you intend soon to resign your liberty forever, and come under a despotism of the most cruel and inexorable character, you must abandon the morning bitters, the noontide stimulant, and the evening bowl.

Do any of you drink in secret, because you are unwilling your friends or the world should know how much you drink? You might as well cut loose in a frail boat before a hurricane, and expect safety: you are gone, gone irretrievably, if you do not stop.

Are you accustomed to drink, when opportunities present, as much as you can bear without any public tokens of inebriation? You are an intemperate man now, and unless you check the habit, you will become rapidly more and more intemperate, until concealment becomes impossible.

Do your eyes, in any instance, begin to trouble you by their weakness or inflammation? If you are in the habit of drinking ardent spirits daily, you need not ask the physician what is the matter—nor inquire for eye water. Your redness of eyes is produced by intemperance; and abstinence, and that only, will cure them. It may be well for every man who drinks daily, to look in the glass often, that he may see in his own face the signals of distress, which abused nature holds out one after another, and too often holds out in vain.

Do any of you find a tremour of the hand coming upon you, and sinking of spirits, and loss of appetite in the morning? Nature is failing, and giving to you timely admonition of her distress.

Do the pains of a disordered stomach, and blistered tongue and lip, begin to torment you? You are far advanced in the work of self-destruction—a few more years will probably finish it.

SERMON III.

THE EVILS OF INTEMPERANCE.

HABAKKUK, ii. 9—11, 15, 16.

Wo to him that coveteth an evil covetousness to his house, that he may set his nest on high, that he may be delivered from the power of evil! Thou hast consulted shame to thy house by cutting off many people, and hast sinned against thy soul. For the stone shall cry out of the wall, and the beam out of the timber shall answer it.

Wo unto him that giveth his neighbor drink, that puttest thy bottle to him, and makest him drunken also, that thou mayest look on their nakedness! Thou art filled with shame for glory: drink thou also, and let thy foreskin be uncovered: the cup of the LORD's right hand shall be turned unto thee, and shameful spewing shall be on thy glory.

IN the preceding discourses we have illustrated THE NATURE, THE OCCASIONS, AND THE SYMPTOMS OF INTEMPERANCE.

In this discourse we propose to illustrate THE EVILS OF INTEMPERANCE.

The physical and moral influence of this sin upon its victims, has of necessity been disclosed in giving an account of the causes and symptoms of this criminal disease. We shall therefore take a more comprehensive view of the subject, and consider the effect of intemperance upon national prosperity. To this view of the subject the text leads us. It announces the general principle, that communities which rise by a violation of the laws of humanity and equity, shall not prosper, and especially that wealth amassed by promoting intemperance, will bring upon the community intemperance, and poverty, and shame, as a providential retribution.

1. The effects of intemperance upon the health and physical energies of a nation, are not to be overlooked, or lightly esteemed.

No fact is more certain than the transmission of temperament and of physical constitution, according to the predominant moral condition of society, from age to age. Luxury produces effeminacy, and transmits to other generations imbecility and disease. Bring up the generation of the Romans who carried victory over the world, and place them beside the effeminate Italians of the present day, and the effect of crime upon constitution will be sufficiently apparent. Excesses unmake the man. The stature dwindles, the joints are loosely compacted, and the muscular fibre has lost its elastic tone. No giant's bones will be found in the cemeteries of a nation, over whom, for centuries, the waves of intemperance have rolled; and no unwieldy iron armour, the annoyance and defence of other days, will be dug up as memorials of departed glory.

The duration of human life, and the relative amount of health or disease, will manifestly vary according to the amount of ardent spirits consumed in the land. Even now, no small proportion of the deaths which annually make up our national bills of mortality, are cases of those who have been brought to an untimely end, and who have, directly or indirectly, fallen victims to the deleterious influence of ardent spirits; fulfilling, with fearful accuracy, the prediction, "the wicked shall not live out half their days." As the jackal follows the lion to prey upon the slain, so do disease and death wait on the footsteps of inebriation. The free and universal use of intoxicating liquors for a few centuries cannot fail to bring down our race from the majestic, athletic forms of our Fathers, to the similitude of a despicable and puny race of men. Already the commencement of the decline is manifest, and the consummation of it, should the causes continue, will not linger.

2. The injurious influence of general intemperance upon national intellect, is equally certain, and not less to be deprecated.

To the action of a powerful mind, a vigorous muscular frame is, as a general rule, indispensable. Like heavy ordnance, the mind, in its efforts, recoils on the body, and will soon shake down a puny frame. The mental action and physical reaction must be equal—or, finding her energies unsustained, the mind itself becomes discouraged, and falls into despondency and imbecility. The flow of animal spirits, the fire and vigor of the imagination, the fulness and power of feeling, the comprehension and grasp of thought, the fire of the eye, the tones of the voice, and the electrical energy of utterance, all depend upon the healthful and vigorous tone of the animal system, and by whatever means the body is unstrung, the spirit languishes. Cæsar, when he had a fever once, and cried " give me some drink, Titinius," was not that god who afterwards overturned the republic, and reigned without a rival—and Bonaparte, it has been said, lost the Russian campaign by a fever. The greatest poets and orators who stand on the records of immortality, flourished in the iron age, before the habits of effeminacy had unharnessed the body and unstrung the mind. This is true of Homer, and Demosthenes, and Milton; and if Virgil and Cicero are to be classed with them, it is not without a manifest abatement of vigor for beauty, produced by the progress of voluptuousness in the age in which they lived.

The giant writers of Scotland are, some of them, men of threescore and ten, who still go forth to the athletic sports of their youthful days with undiminished elasticity. The taper fingers of modern effeminacy never wielded such a pen as these men wield, and never will.

The taste may be cultivated in alliance with effeminacy, and music may flourish, while all that is manly is upon the decline, and there may be some fitful flashes of imagination in poetry, which are the offspring of a capricious, nervous excitability—and perhaps there may be sometimes an unimpassioned stillness of soul in a feeble body, which shall capacitate for simple intellectual discrimination. But that fulness of soul, and diversified energy of mind, which is indispensable to national talent in all its diversified application, can be found only in alliance with an undebased and vigorous muscular system.

The history of the world confirms this conclusion. Egypt, once at the head of nations, has, under the weight of her own effeminacy, gone down to the dust. The victories of Greece let in upon her the luxuries of the east, and covered her glory with a night of ages. And Rome, whose iron foot trode down the nations, and shook the earth, witnessed in her latter days—faintness of heart—and the shield of the mighty vilely cast away.

3. The effect of intemperance upon the military prowess of a nation, cannot but be great and evil. The mortality in the seasoning of recruits, already half destroyed by intemperance, will be double to that experienced among hardy and temperate men.

If in the early wars of our country the mortality of the camp had been as great as it has been since intemperance has facilitated the raising of recruits, New England would have been depopulated, Philip had remained lord of his wilderness, or the French had driven our Fathers into the sea, extending from Canada to Cape Horn the empire of despotism and superstition.

An army, whose energy in conflict depends on the excitement of ardent spirits, cannot possess the coolness nor sustain the shock of a powerful onset, like an army of determined, temperate men. It was the religious principle and temperance of Cromwell's army, that made it terrible to the licentious troops of Charles the First.

4. The effect of intemperance upon the patriotism of a nation is neither obscure nor doubtful. When excess has despoiled the man of the natural affections of husband, father, brother, and friend, and thrust him down to the condition of an animal; we are not to expect of him comprehensive views, and a disinterested regard for his country. His patriotism may serve as a theme of sinister profession, or inebriate boasting. But, what is the patriotism which loves only in words, and in general, and violates in detail all the relative duties on which the welfare of country depends!

The man might as well talk of justice and mercy, who robs and murders upon the highway, as he whose example is pestiferous, and whose presence withers the tender charities of life, and perpetuates weeping, lamentation, and wo. A nation of drunkards would constitute a hell.

5. Upon the national conscience or moral principle the effects of intemperance are deadly.

It obliterates the fear of the Lord, and a sense of accountability, paralyses the power of conscience, and hardens the heart, and turns out upon society a sordid, selfish, ferocious animal.

6. Upon national industry the effects of intemperance are manifest and mischievous.

The results of national industry depend on the amount of well-directed intellectual and physical power. But intemperance paralyses and prevents both these springs of human action.

In the inventory of national loss by intemperance, may be set down—the labor prevented by indolence, by debility, by sickness, by quarrels and litigation, by gambling and idleness, by mistakes and misdirected effort, by improvidence and wastefulness, and by the shortened date of human life and activity. Little wastes in great establishments constantly occurring may defeat the energies of a mighty capital. But where the intellectual and muscular energies are raised to the working point daily by ardent spirits, until the agriculture, and commerce, and arts of a nation move on by the power of artificial stimulus, that moral power cannot be maintained, which will guaranty fidelity, and that physical power cannot be preserved and well directed, which will ensure national prosperity. The nation whose immense enterprise is thrust forward by the stimulus of ardent spirits, cannot ultimately escape debility and bankruptcy.

When we behold an individual cut off in youth, or in middle age, or witness the waning energies, improvidence, and unfaithfulness of a neighbor, it is but a single instance, and we become accustomed to it; but such instances are multiplying in our land in every direction, and are to be found in every department of labor, and the amount of earnings prevented or squandered is incalculable: to all which must be added the accumulating and frightful expense incurred for the support of those and their families, whom intemperance has made paupers. In every city and town the poor-tax, created chiefly by intemperance, is augmenting. The receptacles for the poor are becoming too strait for their accommodation. We must pull them down and build greater to provide accommodations for the votaries of inebriation; for the frequency of going upon the town has taken away the reluctance of pride, and destroyed the motives to providence which the fear of poverty and suffering once supplied. The prospect of a destitute old age, or of a suffering family, no longer troubles the vicious portion of our community. They drink up their daily earnings, and bless God for the poor-house, and begin to look upon it as, of right, the drunkard's home, and contrive to arrive thither as early as idleness and excess will give them a passport to this sinecure of vice. Thus is the insatiable destroyer of industry marching through the land, rearing poor-houses, and augmenting taxation: night and day, with sleepless activity, squandering property, cutting the sinews of industry, undermining vigor, engendering disease, paralysing intellect, impairing moral principle, cutting short the date of life, and rolling up a national debt, invisible, but real and terrific as the debt of England· continually transferring larger and larger bodies of men, from the class of contributors to the national income, to the class of worthless consumers.

Add the loss sustained by the subtraction of labor, and the shortened date of life, to the expense of sustaining the poor, created by intemperance; and the nation is now taxed annually more than the expense which would be requisite for the maintenance of government, and for the support of all our schools and colleges, and all the religious instruction of the nation. Already a portion of the entire capital of the nation is mortgaged for the support of drunkards. There seems to be no other fast property in the land, but this inheritance of the intemperate: all other riches may make to themselves wings and fly away. But until the nation is bankrupt, according to the laws of the State, the drunkard and his family must have a home. Should the pauperism of crime augment in this country as it has done for a few years past, there is nothing to stop the frightful results which have come upon England, where property is abandoned in some parishes, because the poor-tax exceeds the annual income. You who are husbandmen, are accustomed to feel as if your houses and lands were wholly your own; but if you will ascertain the per centage of annual taxation levied on your property for the support of the intemperate, you will perceive how much of your capital is held by drunkards, by a tenure as sure as if held under mortgages, or deeds of warranty. Your widows and children do not take by descent more certainly, than the most profligate and worthless part of the community. Every intemperate and idle man, whom you behold tottering about the streets and steeping himself at the stores, regards your houses and lands as pledged to take care of him,—puts his hands deep, annually, into your pockets, and eats his bread in the sweat of your brows, instead of his own: and with marvellous good nature you bear it. If a robber should break loose on the highway, to levy taxation, an armed force would be raised to hunt him from society. But the tippler may do it fearlessly, in open day, and not a voice is raised, not a finger is lifted.

The effects of intemperance upon civil liberty may not be lightly passed over.

It is admitted that intelligence and virtue are the pillars of republican institutions, and that the illumination of schools, and the moral power of religious institutions, are indispensable to produce this intelligence and virtue.

But who are found so uniformly in the ranks of irreligion as the intemperate? Who like these violate the Sabbath, and set their mouth against the heavens—neglecting the education of their families—and corrupting their morals? Almost the entire amount of national ignorance and crime is the offspring of intemperance. Throughout the land, the intemperate are hewing down the pillars, and undermining the foundations of our national edifice. Legions have besieged it, and upon every gate the battle-axe rings; and still the sentinels sleep.

Should the evil advance as it has done, the day is not far distant when the great body of the laboring classes of the community, the bones and sinews of the nation, will be contaminated; and when this is accomplished, the right of suffrage becomes the engine of self-destruction. For the laboring classes constitute an immense majority, and when these are perverted by intemperance, ambition needs no better implements with which to dig the grave of our liberties, and entomb our glory.

Such is the influence of interest, ambition, fear, and indolence, that one violent partisan, with a handful of disciplined troops, may overrule the influence of five hundred temperate men, who act without concert. Already is the disposition to temporize, to tolerate, and even to court the intemperate, too apparent, on account of the apprehended retribution of their perverted suffrage. The whole power of law, through the nation, sleeps in the statute book, and until public sentiment is roused and concentrated, it may be doubted whether its execution is possible.

Where is the city, town, or village, in which the laws are not openly violated, and where is the magistracy that dares to carry into effect the laws against the vending or drinking of ardent spirits? Here then an aristocracy of bad influence has already risen up, which bids defiance to law, and threatens the extirpation of civil liberty. As intemperance increases, the power of taxation will come more and more into the hands of men of intemperate habits and desperate fortunes; of course the laws gradually will become subservient to the debtor, and less efficacious in protecting the rights of property. This will be a vital stab to liberty—to the security of which property is indispensable. For money is the sinew of war—and when those who hold the property of a nation cannot be protected in their rights, they will change the form of government, peaceably if they may, by violence if they must.

In proportion to the numbers who have no right in the soil, and no capital at stake, and no moral principle, will the nation be exposed to violence and revolution. In Europe, the physical power is bereft of the right of suffrage, and by the bayonet is kept down. But in this nation, the power which may be wielded by the intemperate and ignorant is tremendous. These are the troops of the future Cæsars, by whose perverted suffrages our future elections may be swayed, and ultimately our liberties destroyed. They are the corps of irreligious and desperate men, who have something to hope, and nothing to fear, from revolution and blood. Of such materials was the army of Catiline composed, who conspired against the liberties of Rome. And in the French revolution, such men as Lafayette were soon swept from the helm, by mobs composed of the dregs of creation, to give place to the revolutionary furies which followed.

We boast of our liberties, and rejoice in our prospective instrumentality in disenthralling the world. But our own foundations rest on the heaving sides of a burning mountain, through which, in thousands of places, the fire has burst out, and is blazing around us. If they cannot be extinguished, we are undone. Our sun is fast setting, and the darkness of an endless night is closing in upon us.

SERMON IV.

THE REMEDY OF INTEMPERANCE.

HABAKKUK, ii. 9—11, 15, 16.

Wo to him that coveteth an evil covetousness to his house, that he may set his nest on high, that he may be delivered from the power of evil! Thou hast consulted shame to thy house by cutting off many people, and hast sinned against thy soul. For the stone shall cry out of the wall, and the beam out of the timber shall answer it.
Wo unto him that giveth his neighbor drink, that puttest thy bottle to him, and makest him drunken also, that thou mayest look on their nakedness! Thou art filled with shame for glory: drink thou also, and let thy foreskin be uncovered: the cup of the LORD's right hand shall be turned unto thee, and shameful spewing shall be on thy glory.

WE now come to the inquiry, BY WHAT MEANS CAN THE EVIL OF INTEMPERANCE BE STAYED? and the answer is, not by any *one thing*, but by every thing which can be put in requisition to hem in the army of the destroyer, and impede his march, and turn him back, and redeem the land.

Intemperance is a national sin, carrying destruction from the centre to every extremity of the empire, and calling upon the nation to array itself, *en masse*, against it.

It is in vain to rely alone upon self-government, and voluntary abstinence. This, by all means, should be encouraged and enforced, and may limit the evil, but can never expel it. Alike hopeless are all the efforts of the pulpit, and the press, without something more radical, efficient and permanent. If knowledge only, or argument, or motive, were needed, the task of reformation would be easy. But argument may as well be exerted upon the wind, and motive be applied to chain down the waves. Thirst, and the love of filthy lucre, are incorrigible. Many may be saved by these means; but with nothing more, many will be lost, and the evil will go down to other ages. Alike hopeless is the attempt to stop intemperance by mere civil coercion.

There is too much capital vested in the importation, distillation, and vending of ardent spirits, and too brisk a demand for their consumption in the market, to render mere legal enactments and prohibitions, of sufficient influence to keep the practice of trafficking in ardent spirits within safe limits. As well might the ocean be poured out upon the Andes, and its waters be stopped from rushing violently down their sides. It would require an omniscient eye, and an almighty arm, punishing with speedy and certain retribution all delinquents, to stay the progress of intemperance in the presence of the all-pervading temptation of ardent spirits.

Magistrates WILL NOT, and CANNOT, if they would, execute the laws against the unlawful vending and drinking of ardent spirits, amid a population who hold the right of suffrage, and are in favor of free indulgence. The effort, before the public sentiment was prepared for it, would hurl them quick from their elevation, and exalt others who would be no terror to evil doers. Our Fathers could enforce morality by law; but the times are changed, and unless we can regulate public sentiment, and secure morality in some other way, WE ARE UNDONE.

Voluntary associations to support the magistrate in the execution of the law are useful, but after all are ineffectual—for though, in a single town, or state, they may effect a temporary reformation, it requires an effort to make them universal, and to keep up their energy, which never has been, and never will be made.

Besides, the reformation of a town, or even of a state, is but emptying of its waters the bed of a river, to be instantly replaced by the waters from above; or like the creation of a vacuum in the atmosphere, which is instantly filled by the pressure of the circumjacent air.

The remedy, whatever it may be, must be universal, operating permanently, at all times, and in all places. Short of this, every thing which can be done, will be but the application of temporary expedients.

There is somewhere a mighty energy of evil at work in the production of intemperance, and until we can discover and destroy this vital power of mischief, we shall labor in vain.

Intemperance in our land is not accidental; it is rolling in upon us by the violation of some great laws of human nature. In our views, and in our practice as a nation, there is something fundamentally wrong; and the remedy, like the evil, must be found in the correct application of general principles. It must be a universal and national remedy.

What then is this universal, natural, and national remedy for intemperance?

IT IS THE BANISHMENT OF ARDENT SPIRITS FROM THE LIST OF LAWFUL ARTICLES OF COMMERCE, BY A CORRECT AND EFFICIENT PUBLIC SENTIMENT; SUCH AS HAS TURNED SLAVERY OUT OF HALF OUR LAND, AND WILL YET EXPEL IT FROM THE WORLD.

Nothing should now be said, by way of crimination for the past, for verily we have all been guilty in this thing; so that there are few in the land, whose brother's blood may not cry out against them from the ground, on account of the bad influence which has been lent in some way to the work of destruction.

We are not therefore to come down in wrath upon the distillers, and importers, and venders of ardent spirits. None of us are enough without sin to cast the first stone. For who would have imported, or distilled, or vended, if all the nominally temperate in the land had refused to drink? It is the buyers who have created the demand for ardent spirits, and made distillation and importation a gainful traffick. And it is the custom of the temperate too, which inundates the land with the occasion of so much and such unmanageable temptation. Let the temperate cease to buy—and the demand for ardent spirits will fall in the market three fourths, and ultimately will fail wholly, as the generation of drunkards shall hasten out of time.

To insist that men, whose capital is embarked in the production, or vending of ardent spirits, shall manifest the entire magnanimity and self-denial, which is needful to save the land, though the example would be glorious to them, is more than we have a right to expect or demand. Let the consumer do his duty, and the capitalist, finding his employment unproductive, will quickly discover other channels of useful enterprise. All language of impatient censure, against those who embarked in the traffick of ardent spirits while it was deemed a lawful calling, should therefore be forborne. It would only serve to irritate and arouse prejudice, and prevent investigation, and concentrate a deaf and deadly opposition against the work of reformation. No *ex post facto* laws.—Let us all rather confess the sins which are past, and leave the things which are behind, and press forward in one harmonious attempt to reform the land, and perpetuate our invaluable blessings.

This however cannot be done effectually so long as the traffick in ardent spirits is regarded as lawful, and is patronised by men of reputation and moral worth in every part of the land. Like slavery, it must be regarded as sinful, impolitic, and dishonorable. That no measures will avail short of rendering ardent spirits a contraband of trade, is nearly self-evident.

Could intemperance be stopped, did all the rivers in the land flow with inebriating and fascinating liquids? But the abundance and cheapness of ardent spirits is such, that, surrounded as it is by the seductions of company, and every artifice of entertainment, it is more tempting and fatal than if it flowed freely as water. Then, like the inferior creation, men might be expected to drink when athirst, and to drink alone. But intemperance now is a social sin, and on that account exerts a power terrific and destructive as the plague.

That the traffick in ardent spirits is wrong, and should be abandoned as a great national evil, is evident from the following considerations.

1. It employs a multitude of men, and a vast amount of capital, to no useful purpose. The medicinal use of ardent spirits is allowed; for this however the apothecary can furnish an adequate supply: but considered as an article of commerce, for ordinary use, it adds nothing to animal or social enjoyment, to muscular power, to intellectual vigor, or moral feeling. It does, indeed, produce paroxysms of muscular effort, of intellectual vigor, and of exhilarated feeling, but it is done only by an improvident

draught upon nature by anticipation, to be punished by a languor and debility proportioned to the excess. No man leaves behind him a more valuable product of labor, as the result of artificial stimulus, than the even industry of unstimulated nature would have produced; or blesses the world with better specimens of intellectual power; or instructs it by a better example; or drinks enjoyment from a fuller, sweeter cup, than that which nature provides. But if the premises are just, who can resist the conclusion? To what purpose is all this waste? Is it not the duty of every man to serve his generation in some useful employment? Is not idleness a sin? But in what respect does that occupation differ from idleness which adds nothing to national prosperity, or to individual or social enjoyment? Agriculture, commerce, and the arts are indispensable to the perfection of human character, and the formation of the happiest state of society; and if some evils are inseparable from their prosecution, there is a vast overbalancing amount of good. But where is the good produced by the traffick in ardent spirits, to balance the enormous evils inseparable from the trade? What drop of good does it pour into the ocean of misery which it creates? And is all this expense of capital, and time, and effort, to be sustained for nothing? Look at the mighty system of useless operations—the fleet of vessels running to and fro—the sooty buildings throughout the land, darkening the heavens with their steam and smoke—the innumerable company of boats, and wagons, and horses, and men—a more numerous cavalry than ever shook the blood-stained plains of Europe—a larger convoy than ever bore on the waves the baggage of an army—and more men than were ever devoted at once to the work of desolation and blood. All these begin, continue, and end their days in the production and distribution of a liquid, the entire consumption of which is useless. Should all the capital thus employed, and all the gains acquired, be melted into one mass, and thrown into the sea, nothing would be subtracted from national wealth or enjoyment. Had all the men and animals slept the whole time, no vacancy of good had been occasioned.

Is this then the manner in which rational beings should be willing to spend their days—in which immortal beings should fill up the short period of their probation, and make up the account to be rendered to God of the deeds done in the body—in which benevolent beings, desiring to emulate the goodness of the great God, should be satisfied to employ their powers?

It is admitted that the trade employs and sustains many families, and that in many instances the profits are appropriated to useful purposes. But this is no more than might have been said of the slave trade. The same families might be as well sustained in some other way, and the same profits might be earned and applied to useful purposes in some other calling. The earth is not so narrow, nor population so dense, nor the useful avocations so overstocked, as that large portions of time, and capital, and labor, may be devoted to the purpose of sustaining life merely, without reference to public utility.

The merchant who deals in ardent spirits is himself a loser; for a temperate population consume more, and pay better, and live longer, than the intemperate; and among such a population merchants would do more business, and secure better profits than when they depend for any part of their gains upon the sale of ardent spirits. What merchant, looking out for a place where to establish himself in trade, would neglect the invitation of temperate, thrifty farmers and mechanics, and settle down in a village of riot and drunkenness—made up of tipplers, widows, and beggared children—of old houses, broken windows, and dilapidated fences?

I push not this argument reproachfully, but for the purpose of awakening conscientious investigation. We are a free people. No imperial *ukase*, or forest of bayonets, can make us moral and industrious, or turn us back if we go astray. Our own intelligence and moral energy must reclaim us, or we shall perish in our sins.

2. The amount of suffering and mortality inseparable from the commerce in ardent spirits, renders it an unlawful article of trade.

The wickedness is proverbial of those who in ancient days caused their children to pass through the fire unto Moloch. But how many thousands of children are there in our land who endure daily privations and sufferings, which render life a burden, and would have made the momentary pang of infant sacrifice a blessing? Theirs is a lingering, living death. There never was a Moloch to whom were immolated yearly as many children as are immolated, or kept in a state of constant suffering in this land of nominal Christianity. We have no drums and gongs to drown their cries, neither do we make convocations, and bring them all out for one mighty burning. The fires which consume them are slow fires, and they blaze balefully in every part of our land; throughout which the cries of injured children and orphans go up to heaven. Could all these woes, the product of intemperance, be brought out into one place, and the monster who inflicts the sufferings be seen personified, the nation would be furious with indignation. Humanity, conscience, religion, all would conspire to stop a work of such malignity.

We are appalled, and shocked, at the accounts from the east, of widows burnt upon the funeral piles of their departed husbands. But what if those devotees of superstition, the Brahmins, had discovered a mode of prolonging the lives of the victims for years amid the flames, and by these protracted burnings were accustomed to torture life away? We might almost rouse up a crusade to cross the deep, to stop by force such inhumanity. But, alas! we should leave behind us, on our own shores, more wives in the fire, than we should find of widows thus sacrificed in all the east; a fire too, which, besides its action upon the body, tortures the soul by lost affections, and ruined hopes, and prospective wretchedness.

It is high time to enter upon the business of collecting facts on this subject. The statistics of intemperance should be published; for no man has comprehended as yet the height, and depth, and length, and breadth of this mighty evil.

We execrate the cruelties of the slave trade—the husband torn from the bosom of his wife—the son from his father—brothers and sisters separated forever—whole families in a moment ruined! But are there no similar enormities to be witnessed in the United States? None indeed perpetrated by the bayonet—but many, very many, perpetrated by intemperance.

Every year thousands of families are robbed of fathers, brothers, husbands, friends. Every year widows and orphans are multiplied, and grey hairs are brought with sorrow to the grave—no disease makes such inroads upon families, blasts so many hopes, destroys so many lives, and causes so many mourners to go about the streets, because man goeth to his long home.

We have heard of the horrors of the middle passage—the transportation of slaves—the chains—the darkness—the stench—the mortality and living madness of wo—and it is dreadful. But bring together the victims of intemperance, and crowd them into one vast lazar-house, and sights of wo quite as appalling would meet your eyes.

Yes, in this nation there is a middle passage of slavery, and darkness, and chains, and disease, and death. But it is a middle passage, not from Africa to America, but from time to eternity, and not of slaves whom death will release from suffering, but of those whose sufferings at death do but just begin. Could all the sighs of these captives be wafted on one breeze, it would be, loud as thunder. Could all their tears be assembled, they would be like the sea.

The health of a nation is a matter of vast importance, and none may directly and avowedly sport with it. The importation and dissemination of fevers for filthy lucre's sake, would not be endured, and he who should import and plant the seed of trees, which, like the fabled Upas, poisoned the atmosphere, and paved the earth around with bones, would meet with universal execration. The construction of morasses and stagnant lakes. sending out poisonous exhalations, and depopulating the country around, would soon be stopped by the interposition of law. And should a foreign army land upon our shores, to levy such a tax upon us as intemperance levies, and to threaten our liberties as intemperance threatens them, and to inflict such enormous sufferings as intemperance inflicts, no mortal power could resist the swelling tide of indignation that would overwhelm it.

It is only in the form of ardent spirits in the way of a lawful trade extended over the entire land, that fevers may be imported and disseminated—that trees of death may be planted—that extensive morasses may be opened, and a moral *miasma* spread over the nation—and that an armed host may land, to levy upon us enormous taxations, to undermine our liberties, bind our hands, and put our feet in fetters. This dreadful work is going on, and yet the nation sleeps. Say not that all these evils result from the abuse of ardent spirits; for as human nature is constituted, the abuse is as certain as any of the laws of nature. The commerce therefore, in ardent spirits, which produces no good, and produces a certain and an immense amount of evil, must be regarded as an unlawful commerce, and ought, upon every principle of humanity, and patriotism, and conscience, and religion, to be abandoned and proscribed.

SERMON V.

THE REMEDY OF INTEMPERANCE.

HABAKKUK, ii. 9—11, 15, 16.

Wo to him that coveteth an evil covetousness to his house, that he may set his nest on high, that he may be delivered from the power of evil! Thou hast consulted shame to thy house by cutting off many people, and hast sinned against thy soul. For the stone shall cry out of the wall, and the beam out of the timber shall answer it.

Wo unto him that giveth his neighbor drink, that puttest thy bottle to him, and makest him drunken also, that thou mayest look on their nakedness! Thou art filled with shame for glory: drink thou also, and let thy foreskin be uncovered: the cup of the LORD's right hand shall be turned unto thee, and shameful spewing shall be on thy glory.

WE have endeavored to show that commerce in ardent spirits is unlawful,

1. Inasmuch as it is useless; and
2. As it is eminently pernicious.

We now proceed to adduce further evidence of its unlawfulness—and observe,

3. That it seems to be a manifest violation of the command, "Thou shalt love thy neighbor as thyself;" and of various other evangelical precepts.

No man can act in the spirit of impartial love

to his neighbor, who for his own personal emolument, inflicts on him great and irreparable evil; for love worketh no ill to his neighbor. Love will not burn a neighbor's house, or poison his food, or blast his reputation, or destroy his soul. But the commerce in ardent spirits does all this inevitably and often. Property, reputation, health, life and salvation fall before it.

The direct infliction of what is done indirectly, would subject a man to the ignominy of a public execution. Is it not forbidden then by the command which requires us to love our neighbor as ourselves? "Whatsoever ye would that men should do to you, do ye even so to them." Be willing to do for others whatever you may demand of them, and inflict nothing upon them which you would not be willing to receive. But who is willing to be made a drunkard, and to have his property squandered, and his family ruined, for his neighbor's emolument? Good were it for the members of a family if they had never been born, rather than to have all the evils visited upon them, which are occasioned by the sale of ardent spirits.

It is scarcely a palliation of this evil that no man is destroyed maliciously—or with any direct intent to kill—for the certainty of evil is as great as if waters were poisoned which some persons would surely drink, or as if a man should fire in the dark upon masses of human beings, where it must be certain that death would be the consequence to some.

Those who engage in this traffick, are exposed to temptations to intemperance which no man will needlessly encounter who has that regard to the preservation of his own life and virtue, which the law of God requires. All who are employed in vending ardent spirits in small quantities, do not of course become intemperate. But the company in whose presence they pass so much of their time, and the constant habit of mixing and tasting, has been the means of casting down many strong men wounded. It is also a part of the threatened retribution, that those who amass property by promoting intemperance in others, shall themselves be punished by falling under the dominion of the same sin. "Wo unto him that giveth his neighbor drink, that puttest thy bottle to him, and makest him drunken also— Thou art filled with shame for glory: drink thou also, and let thy foreskin be uncovered: the cup of the Lord's right hand shall be turned unto thee, and shameful spewing shall be on thy glory."

The injustice which is so inseparable from the traffick in ardent spirits, evinces its unlawfulness.

Those who vend ardent spirits will continue to supply their customers, in many instances, after they have ceased to be competent to take care of their property. They are witnesses to their dealing with a slack hand, their improvidence, and the accumulation of their debts; and, to save themselves, must secure their own claims by obtaining mortgages on the property of these wretched victims, which they finally foreclose, and thus wind up the scene. And are they not in this way accessary to the melting away of estates, and the ruin of families around them? And can all this be done without violating the laws of humanity and equity? Human laws may not be able to prevent the wrong, but the cries of widows and orphans will be heard in heaven, and a retribution which human tribunals cannot award, will be reserved for the day of judgment. Is it not an "evil covetousness" that rolls up an estate by such methods? It is like "building a town with blood, and establishing a city by iniquity." And can those who do thus escape the wo denounced against him, "that giveth his neighbor drink, that putteth his bottle to him, and maketh him drunken?"

Can it be denied that the commerce in ardent spirits makes a fearful havock of property, morals, and life? Does it not shed blood as really as the sword, and more blood than is shed by war? In this point none are better witnesses than physicians, and, according to their testimony, intemperance is one of the greatest destroyers of virtue, health and life.

It is admitted that commerce generally lays a heavy tax upon life and morals. But it is an evil inseparable from a course of things which is actually indispensable to civilization. The entire melioration of the human condition seems to depend upon it, so that were commerce to cease, agriculture would fall back to the simple product of a supply without surplus, destroying the arts, and cutting the sinews of industry. But the commerce in ardent spirits stands on a different ground: its evils are compensated by no greater good; it promotes no good purpose which would not prosper better without it; it does not afford property to those who engage in it, which they might not accumulate in some other way; nor does it give the least adventitious aid to agriculture, or the arts. Every thing needful to a perfect state of society can exist without it; and with it, such a state of society can never be attained. It retards the accomplishment of that prophecy of scripture which foretells the time, when the knowledge of the Lord shall cover the earth, and violence and fraud shall cease.

The consideration, that those, to whose injury we are accessary by the sale of ardent spirits, are destroyed also by the perversion of their own free-agency—and that the evil is silent, and slow-paced in its march—doubtless subtracts in no small degree, from the keen sense of accountability and crime, which would attend the administration of arsenic, or the taking of life by the pistol, or the dagger—as does also the consideration, that although we may withhold the cup, yet, from some other source, the deleterious potion will be obtained.

But all this alters not the case. He who deliberately assists his neighbor to destroy his life, is not guiltless because his neighbor is a free agent and is also guilty—and he is accessary to the crime, though twenty other persons might have been ready to commit the same sin, if he had not done it. Who would sell arsenic to his neighbor to destroy himself, because he could obtain it elsewhere? Who would sell a dagger for the known purpose of assassination, because, if it were refused, it could be purchased in another place? We are accountable for our own wrong-doing, and liable to punishment at the hand of God, as really as if it had been certain that no one would have done the deed, if we did not.

The ungodliness in time, and the everlasting ruin in eternity, inseparable from the commerce in ardent spirits, proscribe it as an unlawful article of traffick.

Who can estimate the hatred of God, of his word and worship, and of his people, which it occasions; or number the oaths and blasphemies it causes to be uttered—or the violations of the sabbath—the impurities and indecencies—violence and wrong-doing—which it originates? How many thousand does it detain every sabbath-day from the house of God—cutting them off from the means of grace, and hardening them against their efficacy! How broad is the road which intemperance alone opens to hell, and how thronged with travellers!

Why is all this increase of ungodliness and crime? Is not the desperate wickedness of the heart sufficient without artificial excitement? If the commerce were inseparable from all the great and good ends of our social being, we might endure the evil, for the sake of the good, and they only be accountable who abuse themselves. But here is an article of commerce spread over the land, whose effect is evil only, and that continually, and which increases a hundred-fold the energies of human depravity, and the hopeless victims of future punishment.

Drunkenness is a sin which excludes from heaven. The commerce in ardent spirits, therefore, productive only of evil in time, fits for destruction, and turns into hell multitudes which no man can number.

I am aware that in the din of business, and the eager thirst for gain, the consequences of our conduct upon our views, and the future destiny of our fellow men, are not apt to be realized, or to modify our course.

But has not God connected with all lawful avocations the welfare of the life that now is, and of that which is to come? And can we lawfully amass property by a course of trade which fills the land with beggars, and widows, and orphans, and crimes; which peoples the grave-yard with premature mortality, and the world of wo with the victims of despair? Could all the forms of evil produced in the land by intemperance, come upon us in one horrid array—it would appal the nation, and put an end to the traffick in ardent spirits. If in every dwelling built by blood, the stone from the wall should utter all the cries which the bloody traffick extorts—and the beam out of the timber should echo them back—who would build such a house?—and who would dwell in it? What if in every part of the dwelling, from the cellar upward, through all the halls and chambers—babblings, and contentions, and voices, and groans, and shrieks, and wailings, were heard, day and night! What if the cold blood oozed out, and stood in drops upon the walls; and, by preternatural art, all the ghastly skulls and bones of the victims destroyed by intemperance, should stand upon the walls, in horrid sculpture within and without the building!—who would rear such a building? What if at eventide, and at midnight, the airy forms of men destroyed by intemperance, were dimly seen haunting the distilleries and stores, where they received their bane—following the track of the ship engaged in the commerce—walking upon the waves—flitting athwart the deck—sitting upon the rigging—and sending up, from the hold within, and from the waves without, groans, and loud laments, and wailings! Who would attend such stores? Who would labor in such distilleries? Who would navigate such ships?

Oh! were the sky over our heads one great whispering gallery, bringing down about us all the lamentation and wo which intemperance creates, and the firm earth one sonorous medium of sound, bringing up around us from beneath, the wailings of the damned, whom the commerce in ardent spirits had sent thither;—these tremendous realities, assailing our sense, would invigorate our conscience, and give decision to our purpose of reformation. But these evils are as real, as if the stone did cry out of the wall, and the beam answered it—as real, as if, day and night, wailings were heard in every part of the dwelling—and blood and skeletons were seen upon every wall—as real, as if the ghostly forms of departed victims flitted about the ship as she passed o'er the billows, and showed themselves nightly about stores and distilleries, and with unearthly voices screamed in our ears their loud lament. They are as real, as if the sky over our heads collected and brought down about us all the notes of sorrow in the land—and the firm earth should open a passage for the wailings of despair to come up from beneath.

But it will be said,—What can be done?—and ten thousand voices will reply, 'Nothing—oh nothing—men always have drunk to excess, and they always will; there is so much capital embarked in the business of importation and distillation—and so much supposed gain in vending ardent spirits—and such an insatiable demand for them—and such ability to pay for them by high-minded, wilful, independent freemen—that nothing can be done.'

Then farewell, a long farewell, to all our greatness! The present abuse of ardent spirits has grown out of what was the prudent use of it, less than one hundred years ago; then there was very little intemperance in the land—most men, who drank at all, drank temperately. But if the prudent use of ardent spirits one hundred years ago, has produced such results as now exist, what will the present intemperate use accomplish in a century to come? Let no man turn off his eye from this subject, or refuse to reason, and infer—there is a moral certainty of a wide extended ruin, without reformation. The seasons are not more sure to roll, the sun to shine, or the rivers to flow—than the present enormous consumption of ardent spirits is sure to produce the most deadly consequences to the nation. They will be consumed in a compound ratio—and there is a physical certainty of the dreadful consequences. Have you taken the dimensions of the evil, its manifold and magnifying miseries, its sure-paced and tremendous ruin? And shall it come unresisted by prayer, and without a finger lifted to stay the desolation?

What if all men had cried out, as some did, at the commencement of the revolutionary struggle —'Alas! we must submit—we must be taxed— nothing can be done—Oh the fleets and armies of England—we cannot stand before them!!' Had such counsels prevailed, we should have abandoned a righteous cause, and forfeited that aid of Heaven, for which men are always authorized to trust in God, who are disposed to do his will.

Nothing can be done! Why can nothing be done? Because the intemperate will not stop drinking, shall the temperate keep on and become drunkards? Because the intemperate cannot be reasoned with, shall the temperate become madmen? And because force will not avail with men of independence and property, does it follow that reason, and conscience, and the fear of the Lord, will have no influence?

And because the public mind is now unenlightened, and unawakened, and unconcentrated, does it follow that it cannot be enlightened, and aroused, and concentrated in one simultaneous and successful effort? Reformations as much resisted by popular feeling, and impeded by ignorance, interest, and depraved obstinacy, have been accomplished, through the medium of a rectified public opinion,—and no nation ever possessed the opportunities and the means that we possess, of correctly forming the public opinion—nor was a nation ever called upon to attempt it by motives of such imperious necessity. Our all is at stake—we shall perish if we do not effect it. There is nothing that ought to be done, which a free people cannot do.

The science of self-government is the science of perfect government, which we have yet to learn and teach, or this nation, and the world, must be governed by force. But we have all the means, and none of the impediments, which hinder the experiment amid the dynasties and feudal despotisms of Europe. And what has been done justifies the expectation that all which yet remains to be done will be accomplished. The abolition of the slave trade, an event now almost accomplished, was once regarded as a chimera of benevolent dreaming. But the band of Christian heroes, who consecrated their lives to the work, may some of them survive to behold it achieved. This greatest of evils upon earth, this stigma of human nature, wide-spread, deep-rooted, and intrenched by interest and state policy, is passing away before the unbending requisitions of enlightened public opinion.

No great melioration of the human condition was ever achieved without the concurrent effort of numbers, and no extended, well-directed application of moral influence, was ever made in vain. Let the temperate part of the nation awake, and reform, and concentrate their influence in a course of systematic action, and success is not merely probable, but absolutely certain. And cannot this be accomplished?—cannot the public attention be aroused, and set in array against the traffick in ardent spirits, and against their use? With just as much certainty can the public sentiment be formed and put in motion, as the waves can be moved by the breath of heaven—or the massy rock, balanced on the precipice, can be pushed from its centre of motion;—and when the public sentiment once begins to move, its march will be as resistless as the same rock thundering down the precipice. Let no man then look upon our condition as hopeless, or feel, or think, or say, that nothing can be done. The language of Heaven to our happy nation is, "be it unto thee even as thou wilt," and there is no despondency more fatal, or more wicked, than that which refuses to hope, and to act, from the apprehension that nothing can be done.

SERMON VI.

THE REMEDY OF INTEMPERANCE.

HABAKKUK, ii. 9—11, 15, 16.

Wo to him that coveteth an evil covetousness to his house, that he may set his nest on high, that he may be delivered from the power of evil! Thou hast consulted shame to thy house by cutting off many people, and hast sinned against thy soul. For the stone shall cry out of the wall, and the beam out of the timber shall answer it.

Wo unto him that giveth his neighbor drink, that puttest thy bottle to him, and makest him drunken also, that thou mayest look on their nakedness! Thou art filled with shame for glory: drink thou also, and let thy foreskin be uncovered: the cup of the LORD's right hand shall be turned unto thee, and shameful spewing shall be on thy glory.

LET us now take an inventory of the things which can be done to resist the progress of intemperance. I shall set down nothing which is chimerical, nothing which will not commend itself to every man's judgment, as entirely practicable.

1. It is entirely practicable to extend universal information on the subject of intemperance. Its nature, causes, evils, and remedy—may be universally made known. Every pulpit and every newspaper in the land may be put in requisi-

tion to give line upon line, on this subject, until it is done. The National Tract Society may, with great propriety, volunteer in this glorious work, and send out its warning voice by winged messengers all over the land. And would all this accomplish nothing? It would prevent the formation of intemperate habits in millions of instances, and it would reclaim thousands in the early stages of this sin.

2. It is practicable to form an association for the special purpose of superintending this great subject, and whose untiring energies shall be exerted in sending out agents to pass through the land, and collect information, to confer with influential individuals, and bodies of men, to deliver addresses at popular meetings, and form societies auxiliary to the parent institution. This not only may be done, but I am persuaded will be done before another year shall have passed away.* Too long have we slept. From every part of the land we hear of the doings of the destroyer, and yet the one half is not told. But when the facts are collected and published, will not the nation be moved? It will be moved. All the laws of the human mind must cease, if such disclosures as may be made, do not produce a great effect.

3. Something has been done, and more may be done, by agricultural, commercial, and man-

* These Discourses were composed and delivered at Litchfield, in the year 1826: since that time the American Society for the Promotion of Temperance has been formed, and is now in successful operation.

ufacturing establishments, in the exclusion of ardent spirits as an auxiliary to labor. Every experiment which has been made by capitalists to exclude ardent spirits and intemperance, has succeeded, and greatly to the profit and satisfaction, both of the laborer and his employer. And what is more natural and easy than the extension of such examples by capitalists, and by voluntary associations, in cities, towns, and parishes, of mechanics and farmers, whose resolutions and success may from time to time be published, to raise the flagging tone of hope, and assure the land of her own self-preserving powers? Most assuredly it is not too late to achieve a reformation; our hands are not bound, our feet are not put in fetters—and the nation is not so fully set upon destruction, as that warning and exertion will be in vain. It is not too much to be hoped, that the entire business of the nation, by land and by sea, shall yet move on without the aid of ardent spirits, and by the impulse alone of temperate freemen. This would cut off one of the most fruitful occasions of intemperance, and give to our morals and to our liberties an earthly immortality.

The young men of our land may set glorious examples of voluntary abstinence from ardent spirits, and, by associations for that purpose, may array a phalanx of opposition against the encroachments of the destroyer; while men of high official standing and influence, may cheer us by sending down the good example of their firmness and independence, in the abolition of long-established, but corrupting habits.

All the professions too may volunteer in this holy cause, and each lift up its warning voice, and each concentrate the power of its own blessed example. Already from all clerical meetings the use of ardent spirits is excluded; and the medical profession have also commenced a reform in this respect which, we doubt not, will prevail. Nor is it to be expected that the bar, or the agricultural interest as represented in agricultural societies, will be deficient in magnanimity and patriotic zeal, in purifying the morals, and perpetuating the liberties of the nation. A host may be enlisted against intemperance which no man can number, and a moral power be arrayed against it, which nothing can resist.

All denominations of Christians in the nation may with great ease be united in the effort to exclude the use and the commerce in ardent spirits. They alike feel and deplore the evil, and, united, have it in their power to put a stop to it. This union may be accomplished through the medium of a national society. There is no object for which a national society is more imperiously demanded, or for which it can be reared under happier auspices. God grant that three years may not pass away, before the entire land shall be marshalled, and the evils of intemperance be seen like a dark cloud passing off, and leaving behind a cloudless day.

The churches of our Lord Jesus Christ, of every name, can do much to aid in this reformation. They are organized to shine as lights in the world, and to avoid the very appearance of evil. A vigilant discipline is doubtless demanded in the cases of members who are of a lax and doubtful morality in respect to intemperance. It is not enough to cut off those who are past reformation, and to keep those who, by close watching, can be preserved in the use of their feet and tongue. Men who are mighty to consume strong drink, are unfit members of that kingdom which consisteth not in "meat and drink," but in "righteousness and peace." The time, we trust, is not distant, when the use of ardent spirits will be proscribed by a vote of all the churches in our land, and when the commerce in that article shall, equally with the slave trade, be regarded as inconsistent with a credible profession of Christianity. All this, I have no doubt, can be accomplished with far less trouble than is now constantly occasioned by the maintenance, or the neglect of discipline, in respect to cases of intemperance.

The Friends, in excluding ardent spirits from the list of lawful articles of commerce, have done themselves immortal honor, and in the temperance of their families, and their thrift in business, have set an example which is worthy the admiration and imitation of all the churches in our land.

When the preceding measures have been carried, something may be done by legislation, to discourage the distillation and importation of ardent spirits, and to discountenance improper modes of vending them. Then, the suffrage of the community may be expected to put in requisition men of talents and integrity, who, sustained by their constituents, will not hesitate to frame the requisite laws, and to give to them their salutary power. Even now there may be an amount of suffrage, could it be concentrated and expressed, to sustain laws which might go to limit the evil; but it is scattered, it is a dispersed, unorganized influence, and any effort to suppress intemperance by legislation, now, before the public is prepared for an efficient cooperation, could terminate only in defeat. Republics must be prepared by moral sentiment for efficient legislation.

Much may be accomplished to discountenance the commerce in ardent spirits, by a silent, judicious distribution of patronage in trade.

Let that portion of the community, who would exile from society the traffick in ardent spirits, bestow their custom upon those who will agree to abandon it; and a regard to interest will soon produce a competition in well doing. The temperate population of a city or town are the best customers, and have it in their power to render the commerce in ardent spirits disadvantageous to those who engage in it. This would throw an irresistible argument upon the side of reformation. There are many now who would gladly be released from the necessity of dealing in spirituous liquors, but they think that their customers would not bear it. Let their sober customers, then, take off their fears on this hand, and array them on the other, and a glorious reformation is achieved. When the temperate part of the community shall not only declaim against mercantile establishments which thrive by the dissemination of moral contagion, but shall begin to act with a silent but determined discrimination, the work is done;—and can any conscientious man fail to make the experiment? "To him who knoweth to do good and doeth it not, to him it is sin." If we countenance establishments in extending and perpetuating a national calamity, are we not partakers in other men's sins? How many thousands may be saved from entering into temptation, and how many thousands rescued who have entered, if temperate families will give their custom to those who have abandoned the traffick in ardent spirits! And to how much crime, and suffering, and blood, shall we be accessary, if we fail to do our duty in this respect! Let every man, then, bestow his custom in the fear of the Lord, and as he expects to give an account with joy or grief, of the improvement or neglect of that powerful means of effecting moral good.

When all these preliminary steps have been taken, petitions may be addressed to the Legislatures of the States and to Congress, by all denominations, each under their own proper name, praying for legislative interference to protect the health and morals of the nation. This will call to the subject the attention of the ablest men in the nation, and enable them to touch some of the springs of general action with compendious energy. They can reach the causes of disastrous action, when the public sentiment will bear them out in it, and can introduce principles which, like the great laws of nature, will, with silent simplicity, reform and purify the land.

And now, could my voice be extended through the land, to all orders and descriptions of men, I would "cry aloud and spare not." To the watchmen upon Zion's walls—appointed to announce the approach of danger, and to say unto the wicked man, "thou shalt surely die"—I would say—can we hold our peace, or withhold the influence of our example in such an emergency as this, and be guiltless of blood? Are we not called upon to set examples of entire abstinence? How otherwise shall we be able to preach against intemperance, and reprove, rebuke, and exhort? Talk not of "habit," and of "prudent use," and a little for the "stomach's sake." This is the way in which men become drunkards. Our security and our influence demand immediate and entire abstinence. If nature would receive a shock by such a reformation, it proves that it has already been too long delayed, and can safely be deferred no longer.

To the churches of our Lord Jesus Christ,—whom he hath purchased with his blood, that he might redeem them from all iniquity, and purify them to himself, a peculiar people—I would say—Beloved in the Lord, the world hath need of your purified example;—for who will make a stand against the encroachments of intemperance, if professors of religion will not? Will you not, then, abstain from the use of it entirely, and exile it from your families? Will you not watch over one another with keener vigilance—and lift an earlier note of admonition—and draw tighter the bands of brotherly discipline—and with a more determined fidelity, cut off those whom admonition cannot reclaim? Separate, brethren, between the precious and the vile, the living and the dead, and burn incense between them, that the plague may be stayed.

To the physicians of the land I would cry for help, in this attempt to stay the march of ruin. Beloved men—possessing our confidence by your skill, and our hearts by your assiduities in seasons of alarm and distress—combine, I beseech you, and exert, systematically and vigorously, the mighty power you possess on this subject, over the national understanding and will. Beware of planting the seeds of intemperance in the course of your professional labors, but become our guardian angels to conduct us in the paths of health and of virtue. Fear not the consequence of fidelity in admonishing your patients, when diseased by intemperance, of the cause, and the remedy of their malady: and whenever one of you shall be rejected for your faithfulness, and another be called in to prophesy smooth things, let all the 'intemperate, and all the land know, that in the whole nation there are no false prophets among physicians, who, for filthy lucre, will cry peace to their intemperate patients, when there is no peace to them, but in reformation. Will you not speak out on this subject in all your medical societies, and provide tracts sanctioned by your high professional authority, to be spread over the land?

Ye magistrates, to whom the law has confided the discretionary power of giving license for the vending of ardent spirits, and the sword for the punishment of the violations of law—though you alone could not resist the burning tide, yet, when the nation is moved with fear, and is putting in requisition her energies to strengthen your hands—will you not stand up to your duty, and do it fearlessly and firmly? No class of men in the community possess as much direct power as you possess, and, when sustained by public sentiment, your official influence and authority may be made irresistible. Remember, then, your designation by Heaven to office for this self-same thing;—and, as you would maintain a conscience void of offence, and give up to God a joyful account—be faithful. Through you, let the violated law speak out—and righteousness and peace become the stability of our times.

To the governments of the states and of the nation, appointed to see to it, "that the commonwealth receives no detriment," while they facilitate and guide the energies of a free people, and protect the boundless results of industry—I would say—Beloved men and highly honored, how ample and how enviable are your opportunities of doing good—and how trivial, and contemptible, and momentary, are the results of civil policy merely, while moral principle, that main-spring of the soul, is impaired and destroyed by crime. Under the auspices of the national and state governments, science, commerce, agriculture and the arts flourish, and our wealth flows in like the waves of the sea. But where is the wisdom of filling up by a thousand streams the reservoir of national wealth, to be poured out again by as many channels of profusion and crime? Colleges are reared and multiplied by public munificence, while academies and common schools enlighten the land. But to what purpose—when a single crime sends up exhalations enough to eclipse half the stars and suns destined to enlighten our moral hemisphere, before they have reached their meridian.

The medical profession is patronised, and ought to be; and the standard of medical attainment is rising. But a single crime, unresisted, throws into the distance all the achievements of art, and multiplies disease and death much faster than the improvements in medical science can multiply the means of preventing them.

The improvements by steam and by canals augment the facilities and the motives to national industry. But, while intemperance rages and increases, it is only to pour the tide of wealth into one mighty vortex which swallows it up, and, with a voice of thunder, and the insatiable desire of the grave, cries, Give, give; and saith not, It is enough.

Republican institutions are guarantied to the states, and the whole nation watches with sleepless vigilance the altar of liberty. But a mighty despot, whose army is legion, has invaded the land—carrying in his course taxation, and chains, and fire, and the rack—insomuch that the whole land bleeds and groans at every step of his iron foot—at every movement of his massy sceptre—at every pulsation of his relentless heart. And yet in daylight and at midnight he stalks unmolested—while his myrmidons with infernal joy are preparing an ocean of blood in which our sun may set never to rise.

The friends of the Lord and his Christ, with laudable enterprise, are rearing temples to Jehovah, and extending his word and ordinances through the land, while the irreligious influence of a single crime balances, or nearly balances, the entire account.

And now, ye venerable and honorable men, raised to seats of legislation in a nation which is the freest, and is destined to become the greatest, and may become the happiest upon earth—can you, will you behold unmoved the march of this mighty evil? Shall it mine in darkness, and lift fearlessly its giant form in daylight—and deliberately dig the grave of our liberties—and entomb the last hope of enslaved nations—and nothing be done by the national government to stop the destroyer? With the concurrent aid of an enlightened public sentiment, you possess the power of a most efficacious legislation; and, by your example and influence, you of all men possess the best opportunities of forming a correct and irresistible public sentiment on the side of temperance. Much power to you is given to check and extirpate this evil, and to roll down to distant ages, broader, and deeper, and purer, the streams of national prosperity. Save us by your wisdom and firmness, save us by your own example, and, "as in duty bound, we will ever pray."

Could I call around me in one vast assembly the temperate young men of our land, I would say—Hopes of the nation, blessed be ye of the Lord now in the dew of your youth. But look well to your footsteps: for vipers, and scorpions, and adders, surround your way—look at the generation who have just preceded you,—the morning of their life was cloudless, and it dawned as brightly as your own—but behold them bitten, swollen, enfeebled, inflamed, debauched, idle, poor, irreligious, and vicious,—with halting step dragging onward to meet an early grave!

Their bright prospects are clouded, and their sun is set never to rise. No house of their own receives them, while from poorer to poorer tenements they descend, and to harder and harder fare, as improvidence dries up their resources. And now, who are those that wait on their footsteps with muffled faces and sable garments? That is a father—and that is a mother—whose grey hairs are coming with sorrow to the grave. That is a sister, weeping over evils which she cannot arrest—and there is the broken-hearted wife—and there are the children—hapless innocents—for whom their father has provided the inheritance only of dishonor, and nakedness, and wo. And is this, beloved young men, the history of your course—in this scene of desolation, do you behold the image of your future selves—is this the poverty and disease, which as an armed man shall take hold on you—and are your fathers, and mothers, and sisters, and wives, and children, to succeed to those who now move on in this mournful procession—weeping as they go? Yes—bright as your morning now opens, and high as your hopes beat, this is your noon, and your night, unless you shun those habits of intemperance which have thus early made theirs a day of clouds, and of thick darkness. If you frequent places of evening resort for social drinking—if you set out with drinking, daily, a little, temperately, prudently, it is yourselves which, as in a glass, you behold.

Might I select specific objects of address—to

the young husbandman or mechanic—I would say—Happy man—your employment is useful, and honorable, and with temperance and industry you rise to competence, and rear up around you a happy family, and transmit to them, as a precious legacy, your own fair fame. But look around you;—are there none who were once in your condition, whose health, and reputation, and substance, are gone?. What would tempt you to exchange conditions? And yet, sure as seed-time and harvest, if you drink daily, at stated times, and visit from evening to evening the resorts of social drinking, or stop to take refreshment as you enter or retire from the city, town, or village, yours will become the condition of those ruined farmers and artisans around you.

To another I would say—You are a man of wealth, and may drink to the extinction of life, without the risk of impoverishment—but look at your neighbor, his bloated face, and inflamed eye, and blistered lip, and trembling hand—he too is a man of wealth, and may die of intemperance without the fear of poverty.

Do you demand, "what have I to do with such examples?" Nothing—if you take warning by them. But if you too should cleave to the morning bitter, and the noon-tide dram, and the evening beverage, you have in these signals of ruin the memorials of your own miserable end; for the same causes, in the same circumstances, will produce the same effects.

To the affectionate husband I would say—Behold the wife of thy bosom, young and beautiful as the morning—and yet her day may be overcast with clouds, and all thy early hopes be blasted. Upon her the fell destroyer may lay his hand, and plant in that healthful frame the seeds of disease, and transmit to successive generations the inheritance of crime and wo. Will you not watch over her with ever-wakeful affection—and keep far from your abode the occasions of temptation and ruin? Call around you the circle of your healthful and beautiful children. Will you bring contagion into such a circle as this? Shall those sparkling eyes become inflamed—those rosy cheeks purpled and bloated—that sweet breath be tainted—those ruby lips blistered—and that vital tone of unceasing cheerfulness be turned into tremour and melancholy? Shall those joints so compact be unstrung—that dawning intellect beclouded—those affectionate sensibilities benumbed, and those capacities for holiness and heaven be filled with sin, and "fitted for destruction?" Oh thou father, was it for this that the Son of God shed his blood for thy precious offspring—that, abandoned and even tempted by thee, they should destroy themselves, and pierce thy heart with many sorrows? Wouldst thou let the wolf into thy sheep-fold among the tender lambs—wouldst thou send thy flock to graze about a den of lions?—Close, then, thy doors against a more ferocious destroyer—and withhold the footsteps of thy immortal progeny from places of resort more dangerous than the lion's den. Should a serpent of vast dimensions surprise in the field one of your little group, and wreath about his body his cold, elastic folds—tightening with every yielding breath his deadly gripe, how would his cries pierce your soul—and his strained eye-balls, and convulsive agonies, and imploring hands, add wings to your feet, and supernatural strength to your arms!—But in this case you could approach with hope to his rescue. The keen edge of steel might sunder the elastic fold, and rescue the victim, who, the moment he is released, breathes freely, and is well again. But the serpent intemperance twines about the body of your child a deadlier gripe, and extorts a keener cry of distress, and mocks your effort to relieve him by a fibre which no steel can sunder. Like Laocoon, you can only look on while bone after bone of your child is crushed, till his agonies are over, and his cries are hushed in death.

And now, to every one whose eye has passed over these pages—I would say—Resolve upon reformation by entire abstinence, before you close the book.

While the argument is clear, and the impression of it is fresh, and your judgment is convinced, and your conscience is awake, be persuaded, not almost, but altogether. The present moment may be the one which decides your destiny forever. As you decide now upon abstinence, or continued indulgence, so may your character be, through time and through eternity. Resolve also instantly to exclude ardent spirits from your family, and put out of sight the memorials of past folly and danger. And if for medicinal purposes you retain ardent spirits in your house, let it be among other drugs, and labelled, " Touch not, taste not, handle not."

As you would regulate your conduct by the Gospel, and give up your last account with joy, weigh well the arguments for abandoning the traffick in ardent spirits as unlawful in the sight of God. And "if thy right hand offend thee, cut it off. If thy right eye offend thee, pluck it out." Talk not of loss and gain—for who can answer for the blood of souls? and " what shall it profit a man, if he gain the whole world and lose his own soul?" "Wo to him that coveteth an evil covetousness to his house, that he may set his nest on high, that he may be delivered from the power of evil! Thou hast consulted shame to thy house by cutting off many people, and hast sinned against thy soul. For the stone shall cry out of the wall, and the beam out of the timber shall answer it. Wo to him that buildeth a town with blood, and stablisheth a city by iniquity! Behold, is it not of the Lord of hosts that the people shall labor in the very fire, and the people shall weary themselves for very vanity?"

Let the discourses upon the causes and symptoms of intemperance be read aloud in your family, at least once a year—that the deceitful dreadful evil may not fasten unperceived, his iron gripe on yourself, or any of your household —and that, if one shall not perceive his danger, another may, and give the timely warning. Thousands every year may be kept back from destruction, by the simple survey of the causes and symptoms of intemperance. And,

Finally, when you have secured your own household—let your benevolence extend to those around you. Become in your neighborhood, and throughout the whole extent of your intercourse and influence, a humble, affectionate, determined reformer. It is to little purpose that the causes, symptoms, evils, and remedy of intemperance have been disclosed, if this little volume be left to work its obscure and dilatory way through the land: but if every one who approves of it will aid its circulation, it may find a place yet in every family, and save millions from temporal and eternal ruin.

I pant not for fame or posthumous immortality, but my heart's desire and prayer to God for my countrymen is, that they may be saved from intemperance, and that our beloved nation may continue free, and become great and good.

www.ingramcontent.com/pod-product-compliance
Lightning Source LLC
Chambersburg PA
CBHW020151170426
43199CB00010B/992